2022. 11. 7.

Hinduism

What You Need to Know about the Hindu Religion, Gods, Goddesses, Beliefs, History, and Rituals

Contents

Introduction

Religion is a personal choice, and as such, it is interesting to learn more about the religions of the world. Please remember that this is an introduction to the Hindu religion and that Hinduism is open to many interpretations.

The following chapters will discuss the history and founding of Hinduism, the basics of the four main beliefs of Hinduism, the gods and goddesses which are associated with these beliefs, and how to practice the beliefs of Hinduism in everyday life. It will also bring up some philosophical questions based on the core beliefs of Hinduism that will help to guide decisions on life's actions.

Chapter 1: History and Definition of Hinduism

Hinduism is a religion based on the concept of 'Dharma' which means 'Way of Life'. In this sense, Hinduism is more of a verb than an adjective or noun. Hinduism is widely practiced in the Indian subcontinent and regions of Southeast Asia, though Hindus exist all across the globe. It is not credited to one distinct founder, though it is believed to have been discovered as early as 3000 BC where notes on Hinduism were found etched in a Chinese text on western religions.

Hinduism is also known as 'The Eternal Way' as its beliefs direct the life choices of the practitioner. Those who identify as Hindus lead many different types of lifestyles. Some Hindus will lead a more traditional Western lifestyle with a full-time job, a family, and creative interests. These Hindus will practice their beliefs along with their traditional societal duties. They will also most likely adorn their homes and workplaces with statues or photos of their gods, keep a ceremonial candle or incense in their place of work, and have an altar as part of the sacred space in their home.

One of the most notable examples in popular culture of a Hindu displaying his or her faith in the workplace is the character Apu from *The Simpsons*. He displays an ornate statue of the Hindu god Ganesh at the front counter of his workplace, the 'Kwik-E-Mart'. The Ganesh statue does not often gain attention in and of itself in Apu's setting, though clearly, it is of great importance to him. He is shown at times simply gazing at the statue as if in deep thought. This is another reference to the Hindu belief of meditation as a form of worship, and the energy gleaned from the representation of the deity will aid in the meditation practice.

Others who identify as Hindus will take a more extreme path and cast off the acquisition of worldly goods and reject the mainstream ideals of pursuing wealth. They instead choose a life of peaceful meditation and worship to their deities and live in a monastery or in solitude, generally in a setting which is located far from any urban cityscape.

Hinduism contains a wide range of philosophies, concepts, and rituals. The practice of Hinduism is very personal to the practitioner. Hindu texts are classified into two categories: 'Sruti' which means 'heard' and 'Smrti' which means 'remembered'. These are terms in the language of Sanskrit as all Hindu terms are in Sanskrit. These texts are important to the teaching of Hinduism as they contain the principal truths and authorities of the religion, though there is a strong tendency in Hinduism to question these authorities in the quest to deepen the understanding of these truths and carve out one's own spiritual path. All of the rules of the beliefs of Hinduism are known as 'Vedas'. The Vedas are the unquestioned truth and lay the groundwork for the Hindu belief system.

Some would argue that Hinduism is not a religion in the traditional sense but more of a belief system that guides life choices. This is a personal journey, though the result is the same — achieving enlightenment by becoming one with the Supreme Being. The Supreme Being is defined as the individual's Eternal Soul. Hinduism teaches that one is completely responsible for the choices they make which govern their lives, and also that no action is without consequences. These consequences are both positive and negative. Hinduism would argue that if the choices one makes are in accordance with the core beliefs, then one will be rewarded with not only enlightenment but also spiritual protection. This protection will enable the individual to have the strength needed to overcome the hurdles life gives us.

If one is consistently making poor choices, then one will be given poor consequences. Hindus teach that those with poor judgment are akin to demons as demons are self-serving. If one only pursues that which benefits oneself, with little regard to the lives of other beings around them, then their life is void of meaning. These empty lives will go on to create destruction and chaos. As a Hindu, you can recognize these living demons and will have the strength of character not to be brought into their self-serving way of life. This is not to say that someone who is making poor choices could not ever change their ways. Hindus believe that all living creatures are made in the image of the Divine Deities and therefore any living being has the capacity to live in accordance with good Dharma. Therefore, if one makes the conscious choice to change towards living a better Dharma, then one has the chance to be forgiven and therefore is one step closer to living a better Dharma.

Hindu is one of the world's largest religions with over 1.5 billion members. This accounts for close to 15 percent of the world's population.

Hinduism and the Vedas

Hinduism gathers or obtains its philosophy, beliefs, and traditions from several sources. Scriptures are an integral source of religious theory, wisdom, and learning. There are many references to the Vedas in studies and theories related to Hinduism. Unlike other major world religions, Hinduism doesn't depend on a single source of knowledge, scripture, incident or revelation of truth or god to put forth its philosophy. The beauty of this religion is that it is all-encompassing and all-embracing. It borrows or draws inspiration from innumerable sources, from ascetic movements to teachers to literary sources.

Sacred Hinduism Texts

Over centuries, Hinduism has undergone a considerable transformation while drawing inspiration from varied sources. The most important of these sources are Vedas, Upanishads (the latter parts of Vedas), Puranas, Bhagavadgita, Sutras, Vedangas, Darshanas, and the two epics, Mahabharata and Ramayana. Then there is the Vaishanava literature, the Agamas and Dharma Shastras, and the commentaries known as Karikas and Bhashyas. This is just the tip of the iceberg. There are also works of personalities by several prominent personalities, such as Shri Ramanuja and Shri Shankaracharya.

The Vedas

There are four Vedas, namely Rigveda, Yajurveda, Samaveda, and Atharvaveda. As per a tradition, only Rigvedam Yajurveda and Samaveda were given the status of real Vedas. It took a while for Atharvaveda to join the list of Vedas. It is believed that the Vedas haven't been created by man or god. They are a result of the knowledge gained by seers in deep meditative stages. This is probably why they are referred to as shrutis (ones that are heard) than smritis (memorial texts). The Vedic Aryans held the Vedas as classic or timeless, which were revealed by Brahman or Supreme Being. The Vedas are considered evergreen and indestructible elements of Brahman that stay with us until the creation cycle lasts and will be taken away much like all else when the worlds and living beings begin to dissolve. They are the cornerstone of Vedic religion from which Hinduism itself has originated in slow phases. The Vedas are known to be the Brahman personification in a literary form. Hence, they are considered holy and venerable.

Hinduism considers Vedas as the companions of the wise, knowledgeable, and learned. They help people maintain Dharma and achieve salvation. When the Vedas are recited, they bring about purification of the body and mind. It is believed that knowledge of the Vedas makes the practitioner noble, graceful, and austere.

Mastering them is also considered good karma. When Vedas are loudly chanted or recited, their sound vibrations cleanse the atmosphere and are known to make the unholiest of places holy. The Vedas are graphically represented by Shri Dattatreya, one of Lord Vishnu's ten avatars or forms. He is depicted to be accompanied by four dogs symbolizing the four Vedas. The visual communicates that Vedas will always serve the purpose of god like the faithful creatures.

Humans didn't compose or create the Vedas. They are believed to dawn upon ancient seers in a meditative trans. The Rigvedic hymns were mainly ascribed to seven learned men or seers named Atri, Vashishtha, Gotama, Bharadwaja, Viswamitra, Kanwa, and Jamadagni. These names are still commonly heard among Hindu family lineages or gotras.

The term Veda originates from the word "vid", which was again the root word for Video in English. Thus, these were pieces of knowledge as seen in the mind's eye of seers.

According to the Vedas, there are rituals and sacrifices for eliminating impurities or dhodas that arise as a result of a person's actions, accumulated negative karma, birth, direction of vastu related problems, past life problems, relationships, negligence of prescribed duty, improper conduct, illness, association with malpractices, and evil people and more. These rituals may involve invoking divine help, healing restoration, and/or counterspells. According to Vedas, it is believed that performing these rituals according to the procedure, as well as making offerings to please gods, helps gain their help for regaining purity, enlightenment, and mental radiance, while also helping counter adverse effects and impurities. Fire sacrifice rituals are known to be purifiers and hence considered sacred by the Vedas. The Vedic sacrifices of Homa, Yajna, and Agnihotra are believed to be the most effective means of overcoming suffering, pain, and sin.

Chapter 2: The Beliefs of Hinduism

As previously mentioned, Hinduism is based around the Vedas or unquestioned truths. These Vedas could be compared to the Christian 'Ten Commandments' as they are a groundwork of rules or guidelines which the Hindu believes and follows to make life choices. Some of the Vedas are broken down into four categories, all of which are named in the Sanskrit language. These beliefs are broken down as follows:

1. Dharma – ethics and duties
2. Artha – prosperity and work
3. Kama – desires and passions
4. Moksha – freedom from death and rebirth

All of these beliefs work in tandem with each other. While these may be the core beliefs, there are many other beliefs or Vedas that lead and govern the Hindu way of life. Let us take a closer look at what each of these four beliefs stands for, as well as the belief system as a whole.

Dharma

Dharma is a belief and concept which belongs to Hinduism, though it also belongs to religions like Buddhism and Jainism. This is one example as to how many of the world's religions overlap with each other in their beliefs. Dharma cannot be precisely defined into any one language, though it stands for the behaviors, virtues, and duties which bring about 'the right way of life'. The word Dharma is associated with the English words 'law', 'order', 'duty', 'custom', 'quality', and 'model'. Dharma exists in all modes of human interaction, which includes interactions with both living and non-living beings. True Dharma is considered not an act or a result, though it is the natural law that guides the act and brings forth the result. As the Hindu saying goes, 'The sun produces sunlight and the bees make honey'. This means that all life forms work in accordance with each other. With this harmony in work, all life is possible. If all life forms continuously worked in harmony with each other, we would have a world without conflict. The aim of the Hindu is to achieve such harmony in their daily lives, and as such, bring harmony to those around them.

Artha

Artha is the belief which refers to the meanings and essence of the work one does to build the life he or she desires. Artha has multiple meanings that all connect to the activities and resources that enable the individual to build a life of prosperity and function. In our contemporary world, the concept of Artha would be linked to concepts of education, career, wealth, financial security, and prosperity. Artha is also very closely intertwined with the concepts of Dharma as Dharma refers to the work that must be done and Artha refers to the long-term meaning of the work that is done. Without Dharma, there is no Artha, and without Artha, there is no Dharma. This is similar to the old saying, 'Action without thought is impulsiveness and thought without action is procrastination'. Fulfilling the concept of Artha is finding the personal meaning that is behind the efforts done to create a prosperous life one aims to live.

For example, a Hindu will choose to see the work done at his standard nine-five job as an opportunity to provide for his family and give back service to society and his community. Because the work that needs to be done is viewed as an opportunity and not as a chore, there is meaning behind the work. It, therefore, is fulfilling the concept of Artha as the actions are being fulfilled in accordance with Dharma, the duty that is required.

Kama

Kama stands for passion and desire. The term Kama is often confused with the term Karma, though the definitions of the two are very different. Kama is generally associated with sexual desire; however, it encompasses all ranges of passions, longings, pleasures of the senses, and the aesthetic enjoyment of life. Seeking out Kama is essential to a fulfilled life, though when Kama is pursued at the expense of the other core beliefs, this is considered addictive behavior. Addictions to anything will cloud the other senses and prevent the living of the healthiest life. In a world with Kama, we experience love, feelings of community, the desire to show goodwill to other life forms, and create harmony. Kama is also a deity who shoots arrows that will incite passion into their targets. The deity Kama is where the contemporary figure Cupid was derived from. Seeking Kama is what brings our life pleasure and creates a motivating force behind the thought and action that is brought about with Dharma and Artha.

Moksha

Moksha is the belief which is the most philosophical. It refers to the freedom from suffering the cycle of death and rebirth and therefore achieving pure bliss and enlightenment. It is believed that it is to suffer to be continuously reborn because if you are continuously reborn, there is a lesson which life has tried to teach you that you are not learning. To achieve Moksha is a deeply personal journey that could be defined by the word 'Release'. Moksha is seen as the central path to enlightenment with the other three beliefs creating the paths around it. Therefore, Moksha is considered the highest plane of achievement. The term Moksha is used frequently in yoga practice as the goal to be achieved through meditative practice. Moksha is also seen as a state of perfection. In this state, one has no fear, no unmet desire, and no shackles to the physical self. In freeing oneself of these sufferings, one has achieved the state of enlightenment or also known as 'The Supreme Self'. The cycle of birth, life, death, and rebirth is called 'Samsara'. Moksha is defined as the liberation from Samsara. One can achieve Moksha through the understanding and realization that one has an eternal relationship with the deity, that all life is unified.

While all four of these core beliefs are important on their own, they are believed to work closely in tandem. When the proper balance of all is achieved, this is known as 'Purusartha'. This means that one has achieved the life best suited to one's own true purpose and lives in accordance with the beliefs of Hinduism.

There are other important Vedas which Hindus follow that can be broken down as follows:

What is known as Truth cannot be destroyed

This belief deals with the concept that understanding the truth and essence of the universe is what creates the one true reality. The truth may have only one meaning, though the wise interpret it in many ways. This singular truth will always live on. This is one of the slightly contradictory Vedas in Hinduism as the truth of the universe is accepted as the final word, yet there is encouragement at the same time to question the truths and find one's own personal interpretations.

Brahman is the core Truth and Reality

This Veda deals with the belief of the one unified God. Many Hindus know this god as Brahman. This concept is very complex and is a personal definition depending on the tradition and philosophy followed with Hinduism. It could be defined as 'henotheistic' which is a term that means the devotion to one god while still accepting the existence of others. This definition is a little too simplistic to apply to all Hindus, and as such, the definition remains as what each individual defines it to be. One unified concept about god that all Hindus believe is that God is in everything and everywhere. All living beings possess some element of God's divine essence. Therefore, we are all connected, and all life is sacred – this ties in with the belief system of Dharma.

The Vedas are the unquestioned authority

The Vedas are considered the most sacred of all Hindu texts. It is believed that the Vedas were once original texts revealed by the ancient saints and sages. Over time, the physical Vedas were lost, though the wisdom and beliefs that they preached have metamorphosed into the belief system which Hinduism is based on. The Vedas are told not to have a beginning or end like a physical object; they are limitless and will live on beyond any life form on Earth. If the universe were to be destroyed, the Vedas would remain.

Everyone, including those who are not identified as Hindus, should strive to achieve Dharma

Dharma is the concept that dictates the duties one has towards building the best life. This life building refers to the individual and the community. Hindus believe that they should lead by example and live in service to the best life possible. Understanding the concepts of Dharma is the key to understanding Hinduism. This, like many Hindu concepts, is more philosophical and must be understood through personal actions. When someone's actions are in alignment with good Dharma, then this energy will spread to those around him. Therefore, the individuals who are affected by another's good Dharma energies will, in turn, strive for good Dharma even if it is an unconscious effort. This represents the cyclical nature of life and demonstrates how life is all connected.

Individual souls are immortal

In Hinduism, there is the belief that The Soul is the most important aspect of the physical body. The quest for Moksha or enlightenment involves embodying the Supreme Soul. Hindus believe that all living beings have a soul. This soul or spirit of self is called the 'Atman'. The Atman is neither created nor destroyed. It simply exists. The belief is that the journey through life is a series of events that lead to the discovery that the soul belonging to each person is the same soul as the Supreme Soul. This Supreme Soul is the spirit which connects all life forms. This life force is seen as divine and supports the belief that all life forms are divine. This is where the Hindu term 'Namaste' has its roots as the term is defined as 'The divine in me sees the divine in you'. The soul or Atman is the first principle of the true self that extends beyond the physical body. The soul is the essence of an individual. In order to obtain enlightenment or Moksha, the physical self must reconcile with the Atman to see that the physical self is identical with the transcendent self. The soul can be cleansed through the Hindu rituals and prayer. The concept of the soul also connects with the concepts of Karma. The actions of the physical body that the soul resides in collect the consequences of said actions. These consequences remain in the soul, and the soul reaps these consequences once the soul inhabits a new body. Thus, if the actions are poor in the previous life of the soul, the current life will experience the poor luck associated with these actions. This cycle is the derivative of the saying 'What Goes Around Comes Back Around'. The process in which the soul moves from one body to another is called Transmigration. The new body that is picked for the soul is determined by Karma.

The ultimate goal for the individual soul is Moksha

This belief deals primarily with the concept of surrendering the soul to its true divine purpose. This divine purpose is found through a lifetime of making choices which align with good Dharma. Generally, these paths are known as the path of duty, the path of knowledge, and the path of devotion. The path of devotion is seen as the most sacred as this is the path which leads to the absolute surrender to god. This surrender is a powerful belief that guides all thoughts and actions of the individual. Once this surrender is achieved, it cannot be swayed. Achieving Moksha is believed to be the highest gift one can receive in return for a life lived in the best service to the essential life force.

Overall, Hinduism is a Pantheistic religious order. This means that Hindus equate god with the universe. However, Hinduism is also Polytheistic, meaning that it is populated with many gods and goddesses all of whom have different symbolic meanings and powers. This is the way that Hinduism differs the most from Western religions like Christianity or Protestantism. These religions recognize and worship only one true God and have many bible stories about the punishment the one true god rains down on those who choose to worship the 'false' gods instead of the one true God. This is one of the points that causes the most opposition between the Eastern and Western religions.

In conclusion, the Hindu belief system or Vedas are both complex and very simple. The emphasis is to think beyond one's own physical body and to see the world as fully connected. Actions are looked upon as having a sort of 'ripple effect' as the influences and consequences of all actions are shared amongst all living beings and will influence the life of the soul even after the original physical body has left the realm of the living.

Hinduism and the concept of sin

It is important to understand that the concept of sin in Hinduism is not starkly different from that of other religions. For instance, there isn't a concept of original sin in the Hindu religion. It is only known as the opposite of Dharma or not performing one's duty or sticking to the prescribed virtue. So, everything that isn't compatible with one's Dharma or line of duty is believed to be a sin in the absence of the concept of original sin. According to Hinduism, no one can gain freedom from their sins until the Day of Judgment, which means no one can escape hell unless they follow the path of god and abide by his laws.

Similar to Christianity, Hinduism states that sins arise as a result of disobedience for the eternal laws of Dharma or duty. It is challenging to follow all of God's laws, which Hinduism accepts. However, it is known to be an obligation for every person to uphold their Dharma or duty as a service to the lord. When people walk on the path of Dharma and devotion, their mistakes are forgiven. Further, the sins that people accumulate during their lifetime on

Earth can be eliminated, cleansed, and neutralized through austerity and devotion for god. God is known to be all-pervasive. He is known to pervade his own creations too, which are believed to be inseparable to his form.

Sin is known to be an impurity that arises as a consequence of a person's evil actions, which can be cleansed and neutralized through several Yogas along with transformative practices that take one along the path of Moksha or liberation. A person who has attained salvation is believed to be free from all sins. He or she will not be subjected to rebirth or will not assume any more sins. Our soul is believed to be pure, untainted, and sinless. People who accomplish a sense of oneness with their beings or selves become free from sins and pure. At times, God himself is known to eliminate the sins of his ardent devotees.

What is the philosophical concept of sin in Hinduism? In a philosophical context, papam implies impurity, which can lead to suffering, hurt, or injury to oneself. It can arise from physical, verbal, or mental actions of a person owing to impurities like desires, ignorance, attachments, egoism, delusion, and not acting in line with one's Dharma or duty. The primary belief is that if you bring harm, pain, or hurt to others as well as yourself, you are infusing toxins of sin into your body, which will continue to bind you to the unfortunate cycle of birth and death without any signs of liberation or Moksha.

Papam implies sin, which means evil, misfortune, and crime. Our sinful actions can be mistakes, worry or anxiety, impurities, imperfections, evil actions, evil intentions, immortality, disorderliness, destruction, mental. The underlying belief or idea when it comes to sin in Hinduism is that the only way to eliminate sins and cleanse one's soul is by walking on the path of Dharma and devotion.

Chapter 3: The Gods and Goddesses of Hinduism

Hinduism has many gods and goddesses. All are important in their own right and carry with them a back story and symbolic meaning. There are many mentions of a 'Holy Trinity' of gods in Hinduism, or as it is known in Sanskrit, 'Trimurti'. The gods which consist of each Trimurti differ amongst each sect of Hinduism, though many will agree that the Trimurti consists of the gods Brahma, Shiva, and Vishnu. Generally speaking, Shiva is believed to be the one true god across all sects of Hinduism, though this belief is challenged somewhat depending on the personal view of the Hindu. What all Hindus will generally agree on is the belief that God is all powerful and all knowing. The god's true form is shapeless and exists in all living beings. Therefore, all life forms are sacred as they are created in the image of the all-knowing and all being Creator.

Shiva

The god Shiva is known as the Supreme Being. To most Hindus, he is the principal deity of Hinduism. He is said to be the primordial god of destruction and transformation, supreme destroyer of evil and the god of yoga, meditation, and the arts. In most interpretations, he is the center of the 'Trimurti', which is the holy trinity of deities. The other two gods in the trinity are Brahma and Vishnu. There are a few trinities mentioned in Hinduism as according to the sect one is following, though it is widely agreed that the trinity involving Shiva is the highest honored. As Shiva is the supreme, he is credited with creating, protecting, and transforming the universe. The embodiment of Shiva is believed to be in many different ways. Some states that he is formless, others say that he is an omniscient yogi, and others say that he is a householder with his wife and family. The only facets which these beliefs hold constant are the depictions of Shiva with a serpent around his neck, a crown made of a crescent moon, the holy river Ganga flowing from his hair, and the third eye on his forehead. The third eye is a powerful symbol of perception beyond physical sight. This third eye is the path to the gate that leads to higher consciousness. As Shiva is the most powerful deity of Hinduism, he is the creator of this high consciousness. The worship of Shiva is known as 'Shaivism', which is a sect of Hinduism. Practitioners of this sect believe that Shiva is in everything and is everywhere. All creation and destruction results from Shiva. Shiva is called the 'Absolute Reality' as his existence is what is responsible for all life on Earth. Shiva the God is not to be confused with the Orthodox Jewish tradition of 'Sitting Shiva' which is a seven-day stance of mourning for the loss of a first-degree blood relative.

Parvati

Parvati is the wife of Shiva in his embodiment of the head of the household. Parvati is hailed as the goddess of fertility, love, beauty, and devotion. She is said to possess a quiet, divine strength. Her source of worship differs somewhat depending on the sect of Hinduism that is revered, though it is generally agreed upon that she is the Divine Mother Goddess. She is the mother of the god Ganesha or also known as Ganesh. She forms one of the Trimurti of goddesses along with Lakshmi and Saraswati. In the sect of Shaiva, Parvati is worshipped as the source of all godly power along with

Shiva. She is the regenerative force behind Shiva's power, and it is through her spiritual release that the bond between all living beings is formed. Representations of Parvati are very common in Hindu temples throughout India, and as such, she is one of the most widely recognized figures of the Hindu deities.

The name Parvati literally means 'One with the mountains'. This meaning is interpreted through the genealogy of Parvati as she is the daughter of King Parvat who ruled the kingdoms in the mountains. Throughout time, there have been many interpretations of Parvati, and she is sometimes thought of as the combination of all of the wives to the gods. As such, she is known as the Eternal Mother as she provides the life force behind the powerful god rulers. Parvati is depicted often as having two arms when she is seen with Shiva and has four arms when she is seen alone. She is often depicted wearing a red sari with a gold headband. Some of the most cherished depictions of Parvati include her with her two children, the first born, Ganesh, on her knee and the second born, Skanda, playing on the ground near her feet. In the depictions of her having two hands, both hands are held in symbols. These symbols through hands are called 'Mudras'. One of her hands is always in the hand position Mudra meaning Fear Not. This is an indicator of her great maternal strength. Both of her hands are always held in a motherly gesture. There are also widely revered depictions of Parvati and Shiva in sexual union. This represents the union of the 'Yoni' (female energy) and 'Linga' (male energy). This combination of life force energy is the force behind reproduction and is considered the force behind the union of Parvati and Shiva. Therefore, all other reproductions of life are done in their image. Parvati is also often depicted with a golden yellow skin tone to reflect her worship as the goddess of ripened harvests.

Durga

Durga is the warrior goddess. She is known by other names such as Amba and Kali. Durga is known for combating evils and demonic forces that threaten the peace and Dharma of the good. She is the embodiment of the protective mother and will unleash her full anger and wrath in her protection of all life creations. Durga is known as 'The Invincible One' and 'Goddess of Victory'. Durga is depicted in Hinduism as riding a lion or tiger that has either eight to eighteen arms, all of each carrying a weapon. Her most famous depiction is of her defeating the demon Mahishasura who is depicted as a horned buffalo. Durga is revered after the spring and fall harvests in India as she is believed to be the protector of life, and therefore, without her protection, the harvests would not prosper. In all depictions of Durga, she is shown as a fierce warrior, though her face is always calm. This shows her inner strength and bravery even in the face of her adversary. The weapons Durga carries also have significance as these weapons are told to be given to her by the male gods of Hindu mythology. These were given to her as the males saw her as the ultimate source of battle power. These weapons include the conch, bow, arrow, sword, javelin, shield, and noose. Durga has been depicted as having many embodiments, though all stem from the belief that she possesses the abilities to be fierce and terrifying yet also benevolent and nurturing. It could also be interpreted that Durga is an embodiment of a matriarchal ruling as the male warriors recognized her strength as to be greater than theirs in battle and therefore gave the leadership to her.

Lakshmi

Lakshmi is the Hindu goddess of wealth, fortune, and prosperity. She is the wife of Vishnu. Lakshmi depictions have been found on some of the oldest surviving temples of Hinduism. Lakshmi is also a principal figure in the Tamil monasteries. She is believed to be the source of the divine power of Vishnu, and as such, this is why she chose Vishnu to be her eternal consort. The marriage of Lakshmi and Vishnu is seen as the paradigm of all marriages. Lakshmi is depicted as having four hands that each represents the four main beliefs of Hinduism. She will hold a lotus flower in one of her hands as the lotus is a symbol of fortune and spiritual liberation. She is shown as dressed well to represent her prosperity and uses an owl as her vehicle, which symbolizes her ability to move confidently through either light or darkness. This refers to the owl's ability to sustain perfect sight in either daylight or moonlight. The festivals of Diwali and Sharad Purnima are celebrated in her honor. Lakshmi is often depicted along with Vishnu as their union is eternal and she is the source of his powerful energy.

Vishnu

Vishnu is seen as the preserver in the Hindu holy triad that also includes Shiva and Brahma. He is the protector and order keeper of the universe. As the legend goes, the universe is periodically created by Brahman and then periodically destroyed by Shiva to prepare for the next creation. Vishnu is the protector of all of these events. Vishnu is known to take many forms or 'avatars'. He is revered to be the ultimate protector whenever evil, chaotic or destructive forces threaten the world. Vishnu is depicted as having a blue complexion and having four arms. He holds a lotus flower in his lower left hand, a mace in his lower right hand, a conch in his upper left hand and a discus in his upper right hand. He is often seen resting on the coils of a serpent with his wife, Lakshmi. In these depictions, he is believed to be 'dreaming the universe into reality'. These depictions show his relationships to the other deities as Lakshmi is his eternal consort and he carries the weapons that were given to Durga, the goddess of war. Vishnu is known for his triumph in the wars with the demons that brought evil to Earth. Vishnu took on the form of his avatar Krishna and made peace with the daemons, learned from them, then used this knowledge to defeat them. With this victory, he brought back hope, justice, freedom, and good life on Earth. Vishnu is one of the most widely recognized gods from Hinduism as his likeness is generally used to represent Hinduism. Devout practitioners of Hinduism will often display a statue of Vishnu in their homes or workplaces. Vishnu is the most easily recognized as he is the only Hindu god with blue colored skin, though is often wrongly thought to be the only god with multiple limbs. Vishnu is seen as one of the more mysterious gods as he is more of an essence than a physical being. The best word to describe Vishnu would be the Pervader. He is present in all beings, and as such, is generally worshipped while in one of his avatar forms. Some of his avatars like Krishna are so heavily worshipped that they have their own sect of Hinduism.

Krishna

Krishna is one of the most widely recognized names of a Hindu god. Hindus revere Krishna as a teacher of Dharma. Krishna is seen as a playful figure that uses humor and psychoanalysis to mentor his students. Krishna made a promise to humanity to manifest himself in a physical form and descend to Earth whenever Dharma was seen to be going out of order. This is a very widely held Hindu belief that any influential peace giver is a manifestation of Krishna. The name Krishna literally means 'black' and brings with it the connotation of mysteriousness. Krishna is a highly-represented figure in not only Hinduism but in Indian culture as a whole. His reference is seen in many art pieces, spoken gospel, and traditional dances. It is widely accepted that the time period of 3200 to 3100 BC is the time when the physical form of Lord Krishna walked the earth. In this time, he brought peace and happiness to his devotees and created the groundwork of the worship of Krishna today. The birthday of Krishna is celebrated with the Hindu festival of Janmashtami.

Brahma

Brahma is the third god who completes the holy trinity made up of Shiva and Vishnu. Brahma has four faces and is credited with being a creator. He created four languages that he speaks with his four mouths and is known to be 'Self Born'. The legend has it that Brahma emerged from a lotus flower that was connected to the navel of Vishnu. Brahma is credited with creating the four Vedas (Dharma, Artha, Kama, and Moksha) from each of his four mouths. Each of his characteristics is known in fours. He has been given the names of Vedanatha, which means God of the Vedas, Gyaneshwar, which means God of Knowledge, Chaturmukha, which means Having Four Faces and Svayambhu, which means Self Born. Brahma is a god who exists heavily in the more ancient texts of Hinduism, though is not as well known in more modern-day Hinduism. The reasons for this are unclear; however, it could simply be that the more ancient texts of Hinduism are simply becoming forgotten. Brahma still appears in some of the more widely known Hindu mythical stories. Brahma is known as the Creator and is believed to be the creator of the universe on the secondary level. Brahma is well associated with the concept of Cosmogony, the theory of the universe having two levels of creation. The first level is the primary creation of the universe out of nothingness and the second level is the creation of reality. This reality then has two levels, the primary 'metaphysical', which remains unchanged, and the secondary 'empirical', which is always changing. The true reality that Brahma inhabits is the secondary level in which he created all forms in the universe, though not the universe itself. Depending on the school of thought, Brahma has been described as being born from either Shiva or Vishnu and sometimes is believed to be altogether formless. He is generally believed to be a creator who garners his power from another higher god. These contradictions make the origins of Brahman somewhat confusing. It is important to note that Brahma and Brahman are not the same. Brahma refers to the male god while Brahman refers to the metaphysical concept of the ultimate truth and reality.

Hanuman

Hanuman is a god who is most recognized with his face resembling a monkey. He represents devotional worship in his endeavors as a student of Lord Rama. Rama is known to be an avatar of Vishnu who was a prince who brought justice through his strict dedication to Dharma. Hanuman was a mischievous child born to a mother who was half ape as a result of a curse. Therefore, he was given the appearance of the monkey face. Once Hanuman grew up, he gave himself to service Rama. Through Rama, he learned the importance of respect and dedication to one's beliefs. Hanuman is credited as being a protector of all devotees and later earned the title the Monkey King. It is believed that Lord Rama blessed him with immortality as a gift for his strong devotion. He also represents the concept of inner beauty in that his outside appearance is deemed undesirable, though his inner beauty created by strength of spirit shines through. Seeing someone's inner beauty is seen as a trait of maturity and strength of one's own strength of spirit. The Sanskrit terms for this are 'kurup' (ugly) and 'sundar' (beautiful on the inside). Hanuman is seen to have incredible strength and can literally 'move mountains'. His most famous depictions are of him holding a mountain in one hand while making an incredible midair leap. This belief is the basis for the saying 'The strongest of faith can move mountains'. The pose in Ashtanga Yoga known as Hanumanasana, which is a deep split, is named after Hanuman. This pose is said to mimic his famous wide leaps between the regions of the land he inhabits. Hanuman is believed to represent innovation, learning, and reward for divine devotion. In more modern-day Hinduism, Hanuman is used as a symbol of religious freedom. He is seen as a representation of the right to pursue one's own path of spirituality and religious beliefs in that he himself is a non-conventional figure who surpassed all odds through his religious devotion.

Ganesha

Ganesha is more widely known as Ganesh. He is most recognized as being one of the only Hindu gods who embodies the part human/part animal body as he has an elephant trunk on his otherwise human face. The other god who has this attribute is Hanuman with his Monkey face on a human body. His other known names are Ganapati, Vinayaka, Pillaiyar, and Binayak. He is one of the most well known and most worshipped deities in Hinduism. As the son of Shiva, he is bestowed with Divine Honor. The devotion of Ganesh also extends to Buddhism and Jainism. Ganesh is revered as the remover of obstacles, the patron of the arts and sciences, and the divine entity of wisdom and intellect. The name Ganesh is synonymous with 'Beginning'. Therefore, Ganesh is honored at the beginning of the ceremonies of rites and passages. Ganesh is also seen as the deity of letters and writing, and as such, many Hindu students will pray to him before writing assignments or exams. Representations of Ganesh have taken on many forms throughout Indian art, though the one feature that remains the same is his elephant trunk. Some show Ganesh as more feminized and others as more masculinized in his features. Around the time of 1200 BC, Ganesh was recognized as his own singular deity, and the sect of Ganesh began. This is still recognized as a sect of Hinduism today.

There are also some lesser known Hindu gods and goddesses who play a role in Hindu history and mythology. They are not worshipped in quite the same way that the more divine gods are, though they hold important duties and symbolism.

Lord Rama

Rama is one of the most widely worshipped deities of Hindu religion. He is known to be one of the avatars of Vishnu. Rama is the god of virtue, truth, and principles. He is often referred to as "Maryada Purshottam" or he who knows his boundaries and limits. Rama was highly duty-bound and committed earnestly to his Dharma as a ruler of Ayodhya. He is known as the perfect embodiment of a human – physically, mentally, and spiritually. Unlike several other Hindu gods and goddesses, Rama is believed to be a real figure whose life and adventures are chronicled in the popular Hindu epic Ramayana.

Rama was sent to exile for fourteen years by his father at the behest of his stepmother so that her son could become the king instead of Rama, the rightful heir to Ayodhya's throne. When Rama came back to his kingdom after fourteen years of exile, the entire kingdom lit lamps or diyas outside their homes and on the streets to welcome him. This is believed to be the origination of the biggest Hindu festival celebrated all the over the world – Deepawali or Diwali, where people light oil lamps or diyas and hang colorful lanterns outside their home. Diwali is known as the festival of lights.

Lord Rama killed Ravana, a demon symbolizing the victory of good over evil. In Hindu tradition, this day is celebrated as Dusshera or a day marking the victory of good over evil, which follows a nine-day fast by devout Hindus. The nine days fasting period is known as Navratri.

Saraswati

Saraswati is the goddess of knowledge and learning. She represents acquiring wisdom and knowledge of the arts. In Hindu traditions, rituals, and festivals, Saraswati is worshipped as the goddess of speech, music, language, wisdom, and art. Hindus pray to the goddess Saraswati before embarking on any intellectual pursuit or acquisition of knowledge. Hindu students are known to offer prayers to the goddess in school and college on the day of Saraswati Pujan.

Indra

The god of thunder and rain who wields a thunderbolt. Indra is one of the most important deities of Vedic mythology and is counted among the most important present-day deities in Hindu religion. Referring to Indo-European origins of ancient Vedic religions, Indra is the Indian counterpart of European deities such as Zeus and Thor. He is often referred to as the king of gods or devas/divine beings that represents thunder, rains, flowing rivers, and storms. Owing to his stature as the king of god among early gods, Indra is mounted on his white elephant while carrying his thunderbolt. He commanded the divine devas (divine beings) against their enemies, the asuras (the evil beings).

In early religious scriptures, Indra essayed several roles. As the king, he helmed cattle raids against the dasyus or natives of his land. As the god of thunderbolt, he brought the rains. He was also known to have defeated several mortals as well as superhuman nemesis', the most famous being the dragon Vritra, the leader of dasas and the drought demon. In later age Hinduism, Indra isn't as widely worshipped as other gods but nevertheless plays a crucial role in mythological references as the lord of rain. He is known as the ruler of the heavens and the protector of the east.

In the great Hindu epic of Mahabharat, Indra is the father of one of the central characters – the great warrior Arjuna. In the Puranas, which are a collection of Hindu religious legends, stories, and myths, Krishna (who is an avatar of Lord Vishnu) convinces Gokula's cowherds to stop worshipping Indra. Angered, Indra sends torrential rain to Earth, but Krishna raises the entire Mount Govardhan on his mighty fingertip and offers his people shelter below it for seven days till Indra gives in and pays reverence to his divine powers.

Surya

The golden warrior god who is the protector of the sun.

Agni

The god of fire who is invoked in the sacrificial fire ritual of the Hindus.

Lotus Flower

The symbol which is most associated with the gods and goddesses is the Lotus Flower. This symbol carries importance, as the flower is considered sacred to the Hindu religion. The lotus is seen as a euphemism for the 'opening and expansion of the soul' in the way it unfolds its petals. Vishnu is also known as the 'Lotus Eyed One' in a description of his divine beauty. As the lotus will float on the water, it is seen as a way to describe the 'duty without attachment which surrenders to the Supreme Lord' – that is what one aims to achieve through practicing good Dharma.

Two important terms that come up in the description and worship of the gods and goddesses of Hinduism are Yoni and Linga. Yoni stands for the female reproductive energy, and Linga stands for male reproductive energy. Both of these energies are considered divine as they are the direct taps into the life force. They are often shown as combined, as it is only with this combination that all of existence can be recreated. The Yoni is known as nature's gateway of all births. It is also described as a 'pit of incubation' that is a metaphor for the uterus.

The Yoni representations can be either circular or square, though they all contain a center object surrounded by many folds, much like the female labia. The Linga is also known as Lingam and is known as 'the place of origin'. This is in reference to the place of the male seed that must be passed onto the female to begin reproducing. Therefore, the Linga is where the seed originates and can be used. Representations of the Linga generally are phallic in nature as it represents the male sexual organs. The worship of the Yoni and Linga are known as Tantric traditions. The Tantric beliefs are based on a deepening of the understanding of the sexual experience through meditation. This practice allows the participants to become closer and unite as one through sexual congress. The word Tantra is defined as 'Woven Together'. In Hinduism, the word Tantra also relates to the concept of any one thing that becomes complete and is beneficial in several ways to more than one person. This also relates to the concept of Dharma.

Chapter 4: Applying the Beliefs of Hinduism to Everyday Life and the Concept of Karma

By now, we have learned that Hinduism is centered on four main beliefs (Dharma, Artha, Kama, and Moksha) and that it has a rich history. But how are the beliefs of Hinduism practiced in modern life?

The law of karma according to Hinduism is fairly straightforward, though new-age gurus may want to make it complicated and beyond the realm of the common man's understanding. At its core, the concept of karma implies that all beings (and not just humans) are penalized or rewarded based on their acts and intentions. Therefore, good acts and intentions reap positive rewards while bad actions result in suffering, misery, and pain. With more or less the same core principles, the concept of karma also exists in other religions, such as Jainism, Buddhism, and Sikhism. Good breeds good and bad breeds bad is the basis of the Hindu karmic concept. All living beings are a part of the karmic cycle until they attain moksha (salvation or liberation). According to Hinduism, living beings will gain freedom on his or her karmic cycle only on attainment of moksha.

There are references to the principles of karma even in the Quran, that mentions, "Whoever does a good deed, he shall be repaid tenfold and whoever does evil, he shall be repaid with evil." Thus, though the term karma is believed to have originated in Hinduism, the concept is more or less universally applicable across all religions and mankind. It is the basis of life and living.

There is a strong belief that Jesus was also attuned to the law of karma. How else would he agree to carry the karma of his followers and liberate them from the burden of sin? They regretted their actions and saw Christ as their savior, while also confessing their actions before the Almighty. Jesus died on the cross for he willingly decided to take over the karma of several people.

Bhagavadgita (the holy book of Hindus) has Lord Krishna making an identical commitment to his devotees. He promises liberation for everyone who is willing to give him their actions and accept him as the doer while giving up the desire of the fruit of their actions and practicing detachment. The core difference observed between western and eastern religious philosophies is that while in western religions your sins are committed against God's will or law, in Hinduism (and other allied religions), sins are committed against yourself through your actions.

Karma – Meaning and Significance

In uncomplicated terms, the karmic law suggests that an individual's physical, emotional, and mental actions are all binding. Through the path of our actions or the lack of them, along with the true intention behind, become a part of the cycle of birth and death, which ends only on attainment of Moksha or salvation of the soul. Prakriti is the cycle of birth and death that we are all bound to as living beings until the salvation of the soul.

Karma refers not just to actions but also the effects and intentions linked with every action. In ancient Hindu philosophy, Karma is referred to as sacrificial rituals and other similar acts. Karmaknada were all the rituals and ceremonies Hindus were required to perform as their moral, religious, and social obligation. Over a period of time, though, the concept of karma began to be associated with intentions, actions, and consequences that were all pervasive and binding. This was taken a step further by the Bhagavadgita that stated that desiring fruit for one action was also binding. Hence, man should keep doing good deeds without expecting or desiring the fruits of these deeds. Yearning for the fruits of your good deeds was also seen as a violation of the karmic law.

Not just religious but the scientific world also has associations to the law of karma. Consider Newton's law of motion, which states that "every action has an equal and opposite reaction." Isn't the law of karma prevalent everywhere and verifiable in daily life? We have all observed instances of karma in our lives, our surroundings, and nature too that what is sowed is exactly what is reaped.

Our victories and failures are more or less the consequences of our own thought processes and actions. Positive intentions, thoughts, and actions lead to success or positive results. Similarly, negative intentions, thoughts, and actions lead to failure and suffering. At times, despite positive deeds and intentions, we create negative consequences for ourselves.

For instance, a student may earnestly study for his or her exams but still not succeed. A wicked and dishonest criminal may end up amassing a lot of wealth or hit the jackpot. The karmic theory also factors in the rationale for such occurrences for those questioning it. According to karmic law, the present events in our life are not necessarily determined or impacted by our intentions and actions of the same life. They can also be a result of the intentions and actions of previous lives. This logically explains why sometimes there is a clear disconnection in the actions and its consequences. We may be living the results of karmic actions in a previous life, while the karmic actions of our existing life may be faced in subsequent births. There is no escaping our actions according to the all-pervasive principles of karma. If not in the current birth, we are slated to repay the debts of our sins in subsequent births. This is precisely why some bad people seem to unfairly enjoy all the abundance and success, while do-gooders experience pain and suffering despite noble intentions and actions.

Karmic Beliefs and Principles

There are plenty of beliefs associated with karma, one of which states that it is a self-correcting system and binds living beings to the birth and death cycle, which are caused by their yearnings, desires, and sensory activities. Karma is believed to be the cause of the evolution of living beings from one state to another. It is also possible to undo the bondage created by karmic laws via several means.

It is believed that just like every person accumulates karma through his or her acts and intentions, group actions also incur collective karma that determines their collective future. In line with this belief, countries, organizations, institutions, and associations also accumulate karma owing to their cumulative actions, intentions, and decisions of people who are a component of them. For example, if a country is troubled or oppressed by another nation, countrymen of the former nation acting as oppressors collect bad karma and are required to repay for the actions of their nation with their lives. This is also true for countries, associations, and groups that practice religious intolerance, environmental degradation, or financial exploitation.

As per Hindu scriptures, the karmic law is universal. Even gods are not spared from its effects. It is mentioned in some Puranas that the holy trinity of Brahma, Vishnu, and Mahesh (Lord Shiva) have acquired their divine duties owing to the highly meritorious intentions and actions in previous creation cycles. Lord Krishna is believed to have died due to a hunter's unintentional act of striking an arrow in his (Lord Krishna's) toe confusing it for a rabbit. This is said to be a direct consequence of the action of Lord Krishna in a previous birth (as Lord Rama) when he killed Bali deceptively from behind the tree.

Types of Karma

Hinduism talks about different types of karmas that plan out in our lives simultaneously. Here are the different types of karmas:

Sanchita karma – It is the aggregation of all the karmas incurred during previous lives. It implies the burden of our past actions and intentions that are held in our karmic account and which need to be expended at some stage of the life cycle to help us attain moksha or salvation.

Prarabdha karma – It is a part of our total karma that is presently activated in our existing life, which impacts our present birth or life. Based on our intentions and actions, we either expend it or incur greater karmic burdens for ourselves.

Agami karma – Agami karma is the karma that originates from our present life activities, the consequences of which are faced in subsequent births. Think of karma has a bank account held for you by the universe. Every noble or positive action and intention is a credit into your karmic bank account, while every negative action or intention is a debit from your account. All the plus and minuses of the current birth will be faced on the coming births as per this type of karma.

Kriyamana karma – The consequences of kriyamana karma are witnessed in the present, near future, or far away future in the current life.

If something occurs unexpectedly or in violations of our intentions, despite best efforts, Hinduism attributes it to Prarabdha (the effects of our intentions and actions in previous births). There isn't anything that can be done about it. The only way to somewhat neutralize negative actions and intentions from previous lives is to ask for divine blessings and expend the negative karma through present actions and intentions.

Karmic Solutions

We've discussed how the concept of karma is universal or that no living being can escape its clutches. You will be impacted by it whether you believe in the concept of karma or not. The playing out of karmic consequences in your life is not subject to your faith or belief in it. Karma will keep doing its job without choosing its sufferers or benefactors.

When people know about or understand the law of karma, there is anxiety. We realize that we cannot get away with anything and that every action results in a matching consequence in this birth of subsequent lives. People become anxious and unsure about their future. They become uncertain about how the actions of their past and present might impact their future. Since we aren't blessed with a divine vision, there is no way to determine how our future will pan out. How are we supposed to act in such a scenario? Should people simply stop all actions since every action may lead to a negative consequence at one level or another? The scriptures offer answers to this existential conundrum as well.

According to two predominant Hinduism traditions, Saivism and Vaishnavism, we can undo the effects of our actions and intentions through the divine intervention, guidance, and grace of the Almighty.

Karma yoga – While karma implies performing our social, moral, ethical, personal, professional, and religious obligations, karma yoga is about performing these duties with a specific attitude or mindset, where there is no desire for the fruit of our actions and egoism is non-existent. Karma yogis perform actions with desires and with a sense of detachment as offerings and sacrifices for pleasing God. There are no expectations or desires for results. A karma yogi realizes that it is impossible to exist without actions and these actions will invariably lead to karmic consequences. Thus, the only way to protect one's self from the impact of the effects of his/her actions is developing a sense of detachment from them (the consequences of their actions). A karmayogi is bound by his/her Dharma or duty, not desires. His/her actions are driven by a sense of duty and responsibility, not desire or yearnings.

Since a karma yogi doesn't have any interest in the results or fruits of his/her actions, they are not binding over him/her. The yogi also sacrifices his/her ego to perform responsibilities and duties by identifying God as his/her true self and performing God's works as his/her representative or instrument. Karma yoga is said to be simple in implementation and is highly suitable for teachers, scholars, artists, kings, scientists, writers, and other knowledgeable people, who can extend their knowledge about God with a sense of purpose and detachment while also helping other people. Hindu scriptures cite the example of Emperor Janaka as a karmayogi.

Bhakti Yoga – This is another solution for reversing the karmic effect. Bhakti yoga refers to deep devotion towards the almighty. It is believed to be the toughest of all solutions – since only those practitioners who have had a complete experience of their real selves are permitted to practice it. According to ancient scriptures, an individual is fit for practicing this devotional yoga only when one has usually accomplished stability in other yogas, such as karma yoga, following years of rigorous practice and efforts.

While the jnana yoga practice leads to self-realization, bhakti yoga leads to the realization of God. The only way to realize God according to ancient Hindu scriptures is through complete and absolute devotion. When an individual transforms into a true devotee, he/she is overcome by excessive longing, love, and devotion of the Lord. Thus, God is his all and end all or the only supreme force that guides his/her life. He/she perceives God in himself/herself and everywhere around him/her. He/she also sees himself/herself in God. There is no concept of distance from God, and the Almighty becomes the very essence of his/her soul.

In the Bhagavadgita, Lord Krishna explains the relevance and importance of each yogic path in their true order. He imparts knowledge about bhakti yoga to his disciple Arjun on the battlefield of the Kurukshetra only when the latter reveals absolute devotion when the Lord manifests himself in his real cosmic form. Bhagavadgita's first chapter is related to suffering, while the second has references to jnana yoga. The third chapter talks about karma yoga, while the fourth chapter is dedicated to the jnana yoga practice with complete action renunciation.

References to bhakti yoga are introduced only in the twelfth chapter following discussions on divine manifestation and further discussion. Several practicing Hindus today mistakenly term every act of devotion as bhakti yoga, which isn't what it is in its truest sense. Superficial demonstrations of bhakti or ordinary acts of devotion are not bhakti yoga. Simply going to the temple, performing pooja rituals in the house, or singing devotional songs are not bhakti yoga. It is pretty similar to an attempt to get admission into a top university without learning how to write!

Though everyone can reach the stage of bhakti yoga, not everyone will. It isn't for folks who haven't mastered conquering their desires, greed, and attachments. Again, it isn't for people who have not acquired enough knowledge about themselves or mastered selfless living or do not function with an increased sense of devotion and duty.

In bhakti yoga, one doesn't pray to the Almighty for gaining material objects or favors for oneself or family/friends. The devotee seeks God owing to a deep and intense desire for God itself without any ulterior interests or desires. You truly believe that life without God's devotion and grace is futile. There is a tendency to be restless and unsettled until you find God.

Dharma and Karma

Hinduism teaches the concept of religious freedom. This means that if one lives life in accordance with the teachings of Hinduism, then one will achieve enlightenment or Moksha. This means that life is lived with a great sense of responsibility. This responsibility goes along with the concepts of Dharma that are the concept of Duty. The duties that are obligatory to your position in life must be performed with sincerity and selflessness. This goes along with the meaning of the old saying, 'When everyone puts others first, then no one is left behind'. To avoid these duties will cost you your spiritual health and diminish the power of your soul.

Acting in a way that is healthy for your Dharma is essential because with these actions you will be granted a protective watch over your life from the Hindu gods. This is where the concepts of Karma come into play. Karma is not a concept that is exclusive to Hinduism, though it plays an important role in the religion. The basic definition of Karma is simple – for every action, there is an equal reaction. Simply put, if you do good, then good things will come back to you. If you do bad, then bad things will come back to you. Karma translates literally to 'action, work, or deed'. Karma, in theory, is interpreted as explaining the present circumstances which an individual is in with reference to the actions done in the past.

Let us use an example of a businessperson who chooses to cheat his/her taxes and beef up his/her income sheets to claim larger revenue for the year than what was actually done. He/she gets away with doing this for several years. Then he/she hires a new accountant who does not want to take part in this scheme and reports him/her to the government. The businessperson then owes a lot of money to the government, his/her business is foreclosed on, and his/her employees lose their jobs. This would be seen as karmic retribution. It is also an example of how wide-reaching our actions can be. The employees who worked for this businessperson may not have had anything to do with the dishonest dealings, yet still were affected by them as they ended up losing their jobs when the business closed down.

How then would a Hindu respond to an unfair event in life? A Hindu would first look at the actions that he or she is responsible for. If they were not directly involved with the decision to be dishonest about the business dealings, then they have been found guilty by association, though not guilty in action. Because of this disassociation from guilt in their actions, their Dharma is still pure. Therefore, they will go on to prosper and find a better place of work as they do not carry any responsibility of the unjust behavior.

Let us look at another example. A person has a job in a prestigious position with a high salary. This person has the means to live a gregarious lifestyle, though instead chooses to live very frugally and as an introvert. He/she rents a small apartment instead of living in a large house, he/she cooks all his/her meals at home, he/she has pets whom he/she dotes on and takes public transit to work. He/she also saves a large portion of their income and will say no to any activity that would involve spending money that they do not want to spend. They give back to the community by donating to the local animal shelter, plus they believe strongly in recycling and composting household waste. His/her peers think that he/she is crazy and somehow lacking in the pleasures in life since he/she does not eat at fancy restaurants or take extravagant vacations. He/she, however, ignores their criticisms and continues to live his/her life in this fashion. Karma then rewards his/her actions with granting him/her the freedom to achieve their ultimate goal, which is to retire in their 40's. Because he/she stayed true to their beliefs and chose actions which suited their greater goal, he/she was able to achieve their life's purpose even when faced with the adversary of criticism and misunderstanding from others.

Both of these are extreme examples, though they illustrate what is at the core of the Hindu way of life living your best Dharma. With Dharma, which is your duties, comes Artha, which is your action. With Dharma and Artha come the Kama, which is your passionate force driving you towards your result and reward. With Dharma, Artha, and Kama now combined, Moksha can and will be achieved. Through action, an equal reaction is achieved. This all sounds simple because it is.

Ask yourself these questions about the actions you choose in your everyday life. Does this serve my life to the best of my abilities? Does this serve others to the best of my abilities? Will this bring immediate gratification or delayed gratification? Does this serve only my desires or the desires of others as well? What effects will this action have on those around me? Will it affect others positively or negatively? What are my ultimate goals? Will this action bring me closer to this goal? Will I praise or regret this decision? If an action does not work out favorably towards you, ask yourself these questions: What can I learn from this? How would I react differently if I am confronted with this situation again? What could I do to prevent this from happening? Did it truly affect me in an adverse way or am I just choosing to see it this way? If I have now lost something, am I truly worse off without it? Ask yourself what would be the meaning of true Moksha for you? Do you truly feel that the path that you are on now will lead you to it? These types of questions make you truly think before you speak and act and will align yourself with the core beliefs of Hinduism.

Karma is a somewhat tricky concept, though it can be best described as a boomerang. No matter what direction the boomerang is thrown, it will find its way back to the beginning point. This is how Karma works. It will eventually, over time, find its way back to its beginning point. The negative results of Karma stem from the three roots of unwholesomeness that are greed, aversion, and delusion. This is somewhat similar to the Christian concepts of the seven deadly sins: Sloth, Gluttony, Pride, Anger, Lust, Greed, and Envy. If you are guilty of committing these deeds in access, then you will accumulate bad karma. However, Karma also holds the somewhat contradictory rule that all living beings have free will. Therefore, it is the responsibility of the individual to seek out good Karma. This is where Karma ties in with the rebirth of the Soul or Atman. This is known as reincarnation. Karma is not predetermined in any way. The experiences of the individual are believed to be the result of these three reasons:

1. They are the result of a past action
2. They are deliberately committed free acts
3. They are the result of factors operating in the environment

The rebirth of the soul is the soul being 'reincarnated' to a new living host that comes about when another living host dies. A soul will go through this cycle many times, each time learning a new lesson. This cycle is known as 'Sansara'. This reincarnation is not limited to only people. The soul can be reincarnated through animals, plants, or higher beings. It is believed that at some points in history, there have been reincarnations of the highest Hindu gods walking the earth. The only thing that can end this cycle is achieving Moksha. Reincarnation is seen as a second chance at life, which is both a positive and negative thing. This is why the death of a Hindu is seen as a celebration of life and not a tragedy. This is because it is believed that either the soul will live on or the soul is at last at peace after achieving Moksha. If one has continuously made the same mistakes in life, then the soul will continue to be reincarnated in order to learn from these mistakes. If, however, these mistakes are not learned from, then the soul continues to be affected by this bad Karma.

In contemporary culture, Karma has become known as a somewhat vengeful force. Though Hindus do not describe it this way, it is not an entirely inaccurate definition. Many personal stories of someone 'getting what is coming to them' is often punctuated with a mention of Karma coming back at them. Overall, the concept of Karma should be seen as more of a guiding force, not so much as a punishment tool. After all, sometimes, it is the worst mistakes that lead to the most fulfilling learning. In addition, this is where the root of Hinduism comes into play. Knowing that all life is connected means that all actions by all living beings affect one another in either a positive or negative way. If you strive for good Karma or fulfillment of good Dharma, then your positivity will be felt by others and quite likely influence their own good Dharma.

Karmic Testing

Every situation and occurrence of our life is aligned and patterned as a consequence of karma for testing our ability to gain liberation from the lures of happiness and misery. Hinduism urges the practitioner to be responsive to the karma that is leading them. Have faith in your karmic consequences, in the direction they are leading you. Karma is always testing our capacity for rising above situations. What is a normal person's regular response when they are met with an exceedingly challenging situation? Why do I have to face this? Why me? This is a chance for you to learn lessons you still haven't learned before moving along the path of enlightenment and spiritual progress.

There is a long journey to fulfill along the path that leads to enlightenment. Before you embark on a journey on that path, we should learn all the lessons. Without learning our lessons, we cannot realize enlightenment. If we don't learn our lessons, they will keep manifesting themselves in our path. Each time you feel like screaming 'why me?', ask yourself what lesson is held within the karmic consequence that you haven't learned yet. View these lessons on the route to spiritual development. Our present situation is perfectly aligned and created to enable us to understand and learn these lessons.

Some people wrongly live under the notion that karma is escapable. However, only fools believe they can break away from the shackles of the karmic cycle, which is all pervasive and universal whether you believe in it or not. It is similar to swimming against reality or natural law. Karma is an absolute principle. Its functions and consequences do not rely on your belief in it. Similarly, according to Hinduism, no one in the universe can escape karmic laws.

Chapter 5: Hinduism and the Belief of the Soul

Hindus believe that the soul is an eternal, imperishable, unseen, and unchanging entity whose presence transcends our physical and mental forms. The soul is referred to as Atman in Hinduism. It is why we live or the breathing force inside us which experiences everything that happens to us. The word Atman originates from "an" (meaning to breathe). Thus, atman implies "something that breathes". In Hindu scriptures and philosophy, the Atman is distinct from our mind and body and combines with the mind and body to form our entire being. As per Hinduism, an individual evolves or is self-aware to the capacity of being aware of his/her real nature or self. It is precisely this level of awareness that separates an ignorant individual from one who has achieved self-realization.

The soul as defined by Hinduism isn't similar to the concept of the soul according to Abrahamic religious philosophy. While in Hinduism, it is viewed as indistinguishable from or one with the self and doesn't have any attributes of its own, which is why it is referred to as the Self and not the soul. The self and soul are believed to be a single entity that spells the very force of life, according to Hinduism.

Knowing or being fully aware of the self (or soul) can be challenging. A living being may have to take several births and go through several lifetimes before acquiring true knowledge of the soul or self to attain salvation. Ancient Upanishads or religious scriptures mention that knowledge of the self is possible only when a person withdraws all his or her sense from objects into the mind and the mind into one's self. As per the Katha Upanishad, there has to be purity predominance in order to know one's true self. The self cannot be achieved by preaching, intellect, or exposure to Vedas. It is accomplished only by those who are chosen by the self. It is not achieved by someone who hasn't renounced evil conduct or whose senses do not remain withdrawn. Then again, the mind has to be collected, calm, and restful, even when the person has higher knowledge.

Self-realization should be the goal of human existence according to Hinduism. Every other path brings suffering, rebirth, pain, and misery. An individual who attains self-realization transcends beyond this physical world into the realm of the Brahman or ultimate universe never to come back to the cycle of pain, suffering, and rebirth.

Look at it like this: our individual soul and the soul of the universe are two aspects of similar reality. When our individual soul comes into contact with nature, they enter a net of illusion (known as Maya). Maya or illusion weaves its material net around the soul and binds it to corporeality. Thus, our body becomes our soul's field. The body, in turn, engages in actions that are driven by desire, and in turn, incur karma along with a seemingly endless cycle of births and deaths. The trapped souls are also overcome by ego, which is nothing but an alteration of nature. Our ego is capable of creating a feeling of individuality, uniqueness, and separation.

A true yogi's predominant concern will be suppressing his/her ego while attempting to engage his/her mind in contemplating the self with the objective of realizing it. Based on their awareness, contemplation, and knowledge of the current position, he/she can embark upon their spiritual journey of self-realization from just about any point.

There are several paths for accomplishing self-realization, and a practitioner can pick any of these based on the dominance of gunas or virtues. Practitioners with a sattva predominance may pick the renunciation path, while those with a rajas predominance may start with the practice of virtues and restraints for self-purification.

However, devotion is known to be the best path for attaining salvation of the soul. Again, though everyone can do it, very few can practice it because it needs plenty of purity, virtue, and discipline, which isn't easy for everyone. It needs remembering and taking God's name or unhindered contemplation of the self or the subject of devotion. Ancient Hindu scriptures suggest three elementary methods for practicing self-realization – Sravana or listening, Mananam or remembering, and Nidhidhyasana or meditating on the self. The soul or atman cannot simply be realized through knowledge of the Vedas, mastering scripture, hearing discourses, preaching or talking about it. It can only be accomplished through the discipline of the body and spirit, withdrawing senses, and overcoming desires. It is attained only by individuals who earnestly know, strive to know, and are prepared to give up everything until they reach self-realization.

Hindus believe in the concept of the eternal spiritual reality called Brahman, from where our entire existence originates. The fundamental purpose of life according to Hinduism is to understand the truth and our eternal identity, which is the soul or atman.

Here are some beliefs about the soul according to Hinduism:

The soul isn't born and doesn't die. It is indestructible. The body perishes, but the soul remains eternal. It always exists. The soul is the consciousness or awareness of life. It is the master of our existence.

Our soul doesn't become greater with good actions or diminishes owing to bad actions. It is the supreme protector of all beings or the link between this and an outer world that we all access at some point between our lives. It can be a connecting bridge between this and other worlds as well the plane that distinguishes them.

Those who seek God seek the soul by studying holy texts and scriptures through worship, charitable acts, and abstinence from pleasure. Those that find their soul become hermits. They don't ask for anything for themselves. There is complete detachment from and renunciation of worldly pleasure because when they know the soul, they possess the entire world. There is no desire for offspring, wealth, sexual pleasure, or material comforts. These are considered empty desires.

Another belief about the soul in Hinduism is that it can't be named or defined. It is not something that can be pinned down. It is not comprehensible. The soul also doesn't perish. The soul is free since, unlike the body, it isn't bound by desires and attachments. The soul is calm, tranquil, and free from sufferings. It neither suffers nor has a fear of suffering. Those who have attained self-realization or understand the soul do not experience any sorrow, evil, or elation. They are completely indifferent to things that are done and undone. People who've attained self-realization are their own masters and intensely calm, serene, and unaffected. They can view the soul in all beings as well as within themselves.

The soul can move through several kinds of life, such as animals, insects, birds, humans, and so on. However, it is only during the human birth that it has the chance of acquiring the truth or attaining self-realization. The soul has to wait until it passes through a human form to learn the ultimate truth.

According to the Upanishads, if we spot the soul in every living creature, we see the truth. If we spot the immortality in the heart of every living being, we see the truth. If we look for God within each man and woman, then we will never do any harm to them. If we look for God in ourselves, we attain perfection. When we view our soul in each living being, we perceive all actions performed in line with the soul's energy without the soul itself acting. We find the soul inspiring each movement, though the soul doesn't move. When we view several living beings, the soul represents unity. This is when fulfillment is attained.

The soul doesn't have any birth or death nor can it be divided into various parts. It lives in our body, but it isn't touched or affected by the body. The soul pervades even the universe but isn't impacted by anything held within the universe. It cannot be sullied, corrupted, destroyed, or stained. The Upanishads say, just like sunlight illuminates the entire world, our soul illuminates the body. Those who have a keen understanding and wisdom can differentiate the body and soul. They can detach from the body and experience the soul as an entity that's distinct from our physical form.

According to the Bhagavadgita, the universe originates from God and will go back to God, who is the beginning and conclusion. God is everything, and everything is God. Your innermost desires in this birth will impact your subsequent births. Therefore, your deepest desire should be to understand and know the soul.

The soul cannot be known or understood by those who are not pure-hearted. It is truth, light, space, and life. The soul is where all activity originates from according to Hinduism. Every desire, fragrance, sound, and taste originates from the soul, which is beyond description. There is no known description or definition for the soul. There is only eternal joy originating from it.

The Bhagavadgita also says that our soul is tinier than a rice or barley grain. It is even smaller than a mustard seed or millet kernel. All the same, the soul is bigger than the earth, the sky, and the entire universe. Our heart has plenty of space for our soul.

Chapter 6: Hindu Mythology

One of the most widely recognized rituals of Hinduism is the practice of Yoga. This practice dates back to the findings of Hinduism and is practiced all around the world. Yoga practitioners today do not always practice Hinduism as a part of their practice, though it was not always that way. Yoga is a Hindu discipline which trains the body as well as the mind. The goals are tranquility, health, and spiritual insight. Yoga in Hinduism is broken down into four categories: Bhakti Yoga, which is the path of love, Karma Yoga, which is the path of right action, Raja Yoga, which is the path of meditation, and Jnana Yoga, which is the path of wisdom. Regular practitioners of yoga feel that their practice is on par with the path to Moksha as it deepens the connection between mind and body. This is also an important aspect of realizing your Supreme Soul.

Most of the Hindu rituals are performed at home within the family. Rituals are not mandatory in Hinduism though most choose to practice some. Devout Hindus will perform daily rituals such as worshipping at daybreak, lighting a lamp and leaving food offerings to the deities, recitation from religious scripts, singing devotional hymns, practicing yoga, practicing meditations, and chanting mantras. The practice of worship unto itself is called 'Bhakti'. This literally translates to devotion or love of a personal god. Bhakti is considered the Hindu way to achieve Moksha. Most Hindus will create a sacred space in the home which will consist of a structure containing an altar, a representation of one of the deities, which is usually Shiva, candles, incense, which would have a scent that helps to deepen meditation, and a ceremonial floor mat. In this space, the Hindu will find peace and absolution. This is a quiet and sacred space where one becomes closer to the enlightened state. Some Hindus will also recreate this space in the place of work to bring good fortune to the workplace. In order for a space to become sacred, a cleansing ritual must be performed which consists of lighting incense to clear the air and a recitation of specific prayers to banish all evils which may have once occupied the space.

Hindu festivals are celebrated throughout the year as according to the Hindu calendar. Many of the dates of the Hindu festivals coincide with the lunar cycle of the moon. The most notable celebration is that of Diwali. Diwali is the only festival which is recognized across all sects of Hinduism and is celebrated throughout India and North America. It is described as the 'Festival of Lights'. It is celebrated every autumn as the spiritual victory of light over darkness, good over evil, and knowledge over ignorance. Light is used as a metaphor for human consciousness. During the celebration, lights are distributed all over homes and workplaces. The festival lasts five days with the climax falling on the night of the third day which coincides with the darkest night of the lunar cycle. Generally, this will occur between mid-October to mid-November. Celebrants will prepare for Diwali by cleaning and decorating their homes and workplaces. During the climax of Diwali, the celebrants will dress up in colorful robes, offer worship to the goddess Lakshmi, light fireworks, and partake in a family feast where gifts are exchanged. The origins of celebrating Diwali date back to the origins of Hinduism where mentions of Diwali were found in ancient Sanskrit texts.

Some Hindus do not participate in any of these rituals and prefer to practice the beliefs of Hinduism as a solitary journey. This is equally as valid of a way of Hindu life as ultimately the aim is to recognize one's one Supreme Soul and achieve freedom through Moksha.

The most well-known and most widely practiced ritual of Hinduism is the practice of Yoga. Yoga is practiced in many forms and is popular throughout both Eastern and Western culture. Many yoga studios in North America will use a Sanskrit Hindu term like Moksha for the name of their studio. Yoga is known mainly through the definition of Hatha (restorative) or Ashtanga (powerful). There are many sub-classifications of these such as Pre-Natal yoga, aimed towards pregnant women, or Hot Yoga, which is practiced in a room where the temperature is set at 35 degrees Celsius or higher. Many Hindus will practice Yoga along with a meditative practice that they believe will bring them closer to achieving Moksha. Many criticisms of the way Yoga is practiced in today's world exist. This mainly stems from the way that the Yoga practice has been mainstreamed in today's society, and it has lost some of its more sacred roots. It has become a money-making industry with competitiveness a big part of it. The original roots of Yoga are of a personal and reflective nature; generally, the true Yogi will practice in solitary peace. This is following an incarnation of Shiva who is worshipped as the one True Yogi. Many of the Ashtanga yoga poses are named for the Hindu gods. Most notably is Vishnu's Pose or Anantasana in Sanskrit. The pose mimics Vishnu's reclining pose with one leg lifted to the side and the big toe of the lifted leg grasped with the hand of the same side. This pose is said to bring about the peace and love of Vishnu to the yoga practitioner. Also notable is Shiva's Pose or Parivrtta Hasta Padangusthasana in Sanskrit. This pose is a dynamic leg extension pose while the leg is held under the elbow of the same side arm and the body is balanced on both hands and the unextended leg. This advanced pose is said to bring about the opening and enlightenment that Shiva will bestow upon its practitioner. There is also a reference to Parvati, Shiva's wife, in the name of the pose. There are many benefits to practicing yoga. Many choose to do so to gain a deeper connection between the mind and body and also to relax the mind. Yoga teaches discipline in practice through the physical poses called Asanas. The exact origins of Yoga practices remain unclear, though it was most likely discovered during the fifth and sixth century BC. Yoga gained popularity in the Western hemisphere during the twentieth century. In Hinduism, Yoga is far more than simply physical exercise, though it is a useful tool for physical health. A true Yogi uses his or her practice as a tool to achieve Moksha. According to many scholars, Yoga has the following five principal meanings:

1. The discipline one must have to achieve a goal
2. A technique to control the mind and body
3. The name of a certain philosophy
4. With prefixes to the name, it can focus on different outcomes
5. The final goal the practitioner has in his or her own private practice

Now let us take a look at some of Hindu Mythology. One of the most widely known Hindu mythology stories is the story of the union of Parvati and Shiva. Parvati was born into royalty as the daughter of a king and queen. She was revered as a beautiful and intelligent maiden. At the time that she reached adulthood, Lord Shiva lived in a nearby forest where he was engrossed in his meditation rituals. He loathed being interrupted. The king father summoned the seer page of the kingdom to ask who would be a suitable husband for his daughter Parvati. The seer proclaimed that the only consort suitable for Parvati was the honored Lord Shiva. The king was happy to hear this news, though was not sure how Lord Shiva would notice his daughter while he was in meditation. The king brought Parvati through the forest to where Lord Shiva was meditating. He offered Parvati as an attendant to Lord Shiva. Shiva accepted, and Parvati set about her duties to him. Over some time, the god Kama found Parvati and Shiva in the forest. He was out with his wife, Rati. Kama shot a love arrow into Shiva to make him realize his love for Parvati. The arrow struck Shiva and made him look upon Parvati with love. It also interrupted his meditation, and he grew angry. He opened his third eye and its gaze turned Kama to ash. Rati fainted with grief and Parvati ran away in fear. She then realized Shiva's power and went into penance to seek forgiveness for her feelings towards Lord Shiva. She meditated day in and day out for seven years. After this time, Shiva realized her devotion for her and realized that she would make the perfect wife and consort. He appeared to her in the form of a beggar to test her devotion. The beggar spoke poorly of Shiva, and Parvati grew angry. She declared that the beggar was not worthy to speak the name of her beloved Lord Shiva. Shiva then saw that she passed the test of devotion and showed his true form to her. They married, and soon after, Parvati gave birth to their sons, Ganesha and Shanda. Through their love, the god Kama was brought back to life, and he rejoined his wife, Rati. Together, Parvati and Shiva formed the holy union, and all other unions are built in their honor.

Many of the Hindu mythology stories deal with a central theme or lesson of virtue. These are told to Hindu children to instill the faiths and values of moral behavior. Let us look at some of them.

Dedication of Ekalavya

Ekalavya was a young boy who dreamed of becoming the best archer the world had ever seen. The great archer Drona refused to make him his student due to the low status of his birth. In spite of this, Ekalavya built a homage to Drona and practiced before it every day. He became highly skilled and therefore a rival to Drona and his prized student, Arjuna. Drona tricked Ekalavya by asking him to cut off his thumb as payment for becoming Drona's student. Ekalavya did this, therefore, making himself unable to become his dream of the greatest archer. This story teaches dedication, hard work, respect, and devotion to a cause.

Devotion of Surdas

Surdas was a great devotee of Krishna. He was blind. When someone who intended to rob him was following Surdas, he instead stole the anklet of the would-be robber. When the robber demanded Surdas to give it back, Surdas replied that as he was blind, he could not verify the identity of the robber. After this, Krisha blesses Surdas with sight at the show of his bravery and devotion. Once Surdas had laid eyes on Krishna, he begged for the Lord to take away his vision, as now that he has seen Krishna, he wished not to see anything else again. This story teaches the power of devotion and unconditional love.

The Strength of Durga

Durga was created as the most powerful warrior god when Mahishasura, the buffalo demon, defeated Indra, The King of Gods. Durga was blessed as the most skilled warrior and was given the divine energies of all the gods combined. She then defeated the buffalo demon through both physical strength and her strength of maternal love for her fellow living beings. This story shows the power of maternal love and displays the strength and bravery of women.

The Focus of Arjuna

The youth of the region of Pandavas trained under Drona who was the most skilled archer and master of combat. He gave them all the task of shooting a toy bird stuck in a high tree between the eyes. When he asked them what they saw through their aim, they all gave different answers as they were distracted by the surroundings like the trees and flowers. Only Arjuna said he could see nothing more than the eye of the bird. When he took his shot, he hit his target perfectly. This story teaches the importance of dedication and focus when going after a goal.

The Strength of Sita

Rama and Sita were married and then crowned king and queen. They served a prosperous ruling. Rumors began to fly that Sita was impure because she had lived with a man before getting married, even though she protested that this arrangement was against her will. To continue the faith of his subjects, Rama banished Sita to the forest where she discovered she was pregnant. She then gave birth unassisted and raised her twin boys on her own. This story shows the determination and independence in the face of adversity.

The Hindu Epics – Ramayana

Ramayana is one of the two great Indian epics (the other being Mahabharata) that are considered an integral and significant aspect of Hindu literature. Young children are often told stories from the Ramayana and Mahabharata as part of their indoctrination into the Hindu religion as well as to inspire to travel along the path of truth, virtue, fairness, and duty (Dharma). Ramayana follows the life and adventures of Ayodhya's Prince Rama as he embarks on a mission to rescue his beloved wife Sita from Ravana, the demon king. Ramayana is an important Hindu text offering lessons related to duty, righteousness, mortality, faith, and the triumph of good over evil to Hindus and readers from across the globe.

Ramayana is one of Hinduisms' longest epics with over 24,000 verses. Though its exact origins are unknown and remain shrouded in mystery, poet Vailmiki is credited with writing the entire epic during the fifth century B.C.

Synopsis of Ramayana

Rama is the crown prince of Ayodhya and the eldest of King Dasharatha's four sons. The king had three wives, and Kaushalaya was the mother of Rama. Although Dasharatha wanted Rama to be the heir to the throne, his second wife, Kaikei, wanted her son, Bharat, to succeed Dasharatha. She hatched a grand scheme to send

Rama and his wife Sita into exile for fourteen years, which meant her son could succeed his father as the ruler of Ayodhya. Rama willingly obliged as per his father's orders (since he also practiced Dharma and was a duty-bound person) and left for the forest with his wife, Sita. Though he had a deep desire to serve his people, the lust for power and supremacy was totally absent.

While inhabiting in a forest, Sita was kidnapped by Ravana, the menacing demon king or ten-headed king of Lanka (modern-day Srilanka). Ravana assumed the form of a deer, and when Sita spotted the deer and moved ahead to feed it, he quickly picked her up and ran away while Rama and his brother, Lakshmana, were away. With help from the mighty monkey god Hanumana (and his monkey troupe) and brother, Rama embarked on a journey to rescue his wife from the clutches of Ravana. The demon king Ravana's army was attacked, and he was killed after a fierce battle with Lord Rama. Sita and Rama were united in the end and returned to a warm welcome in the kingdom of Ayodhya. Sita gave birth to twins, Luv and Kush, while they ruled over the kingdom for several years. Ultimately, Sita was accused of being disloyal and unfaithful by Lord Rama and was expected to pass through a trial by fire for proving her chastity. She prayed to Mother Earth and got saved. Eventually, the earth swallowed her into immortality.

Through their legends and actions in the Ramayana, Sita and Rama have come to symbolize the ideals of a matrimonial bond (though this is widely debated and slightly tinted when Rama demands that she go through the Agni Pariksha or trial by fire to prove her chastity). Even then, they represent the ideal couple in modern Hindu religion. Rama stands for nobility, virtue, and loyalty. He was known to be an able ruler and protector of his people. Sita is known as the epitome of sacrifice in Hindu legends and culture. There are several references to her in popular culture as a figure whose self-sacrifice becomes the ultimate revelation of her chastity. Rama's brother, Lakshmana, who chose to accompany Rama on his exile, represents familial bonding and loyalty, while Hanumana's exemplary bravery on the battlefield signifies devotion (for Lord Rama), loyalty, courage, and nobility.

As Hinduism spread throughout the Indian subcontinent, so did the impact and relevance of the epic of Ramayana several centuries after it was created. There are references to the epic in several popular modern-day books, films, and television shows. Today, Lord Rama is worshipped widely not just in India but also surrounding countries, such as Indonesia (there are several popular folklore performances depicting the legend of Ram), Thailand, Myanmar, Cambodia, Malaysia, Japan, China, Laos, and even some parts of Europe.

Rama's victory over the demon king Ravana is celebrated as Dussehra or Vijayadashami, a holiday in India (generally during September or October). During the nine nights preceding Dussera, Ramlila is performed on the streets, stages, and community centers around various parts of India. Effigies of demon Ravana are burned everywhere to represent the victory of good over evil. Ramayana has also been a significant subject of many films and television series in India, in addition to being an inspiration for ancient and modern artists.

The Bhagavadagita

The Bhagavadagita is the holy book of Hindus and is one of the most significant aspects of one of the world's biggest epics – The Mahabharata or the legend of the great Bharata. It contains almost a hundred thousand verses, which are segregated into eighteen different books. The Mahabharata is not just India's but the world's longest poem epics. It is three times more in length than the Holy Bible. The stories and lessons held within the Bhagavadagita have had a huge impact on the followers of Hinduism as well as literature buffs across the world. One of the best aspects of the lessons and writings in the Bhagavadagita is that the lessons are as relevant and important today as they were during ancient times. It talks about several aspects of life and living as a Hindu, including the path of

Dharma, family bonds, politics, statesmanship, nobility, duty, and much more. As such, the Bhagavadagita is believed to be an essence of life itself.

The central plot of the legend of Mahabharata is conflict over the right to the throne of Hastinapura by the Kauravas or kuru descents and their cousins, the Pandavas or the children of Pandu. Due to his blindness, Dhritarashtra (the older brother of Pandu) had to give up his right to the throne to Pandu. However, Pandu ended up renouncing the throne and Dhritarashtra took over. The five sons of Pandu – Yudhistra, Bhima, Arjuna, Nakula, and Sahadeva were raised together with their cousins, the Kauravas (hundred in number). Owing to the underlying envy and enmity, the Pandavas were compelled to leave the Hastinapura kingdom after the death of their father.

During exile, Arjuna collectively married Draupadi, while befriending her cousin, Krishna. There is an interesting story or legend behind the marriage of Draupadi with all five Pandavas. When Arjuna won Draupadi's hand in marriage, during the swayamwara ceremony after hitting his arrow in the center of the fish's eye, he excitedly ran to his mother, Kunti, and told her he'd brought something really nice with him. Kunti, without listening to Arjuna any further, ordered that he share whatever he's got with his four brothers. This is how Draupadi came to become the wife of all five Pandavas.

Krishna accompanied the Pandavas and Draupadi when they returned from exile to claim rule of the kingdom of Hastinapura. When Yudhishtra was tricked into losing all possessions in a game of dice by the Kauravas and their evil maternal uncle (Shakuni mama), the Pandavas were forced to withdraw into the forest for thirteen years. During the game of dice, Yudshistra lost everything and had nothing more to lose but wanted to win back everything he has lost and hence decided to play further. When he had nothing more to wage, the Kauravas suggested that he placed the Pandavas wife, Draupati, as a wage. Yudhistira agreed to place Draupadi as a wage in the last-ditch attempt to win the kingdom of Hastinapura. However, having being tricked earlier, he was tricked yet again by Shakuni mama and lost Draupadi as well. This is when Dhushasana, the younger brother of Duryodhana publically attempted to disrobe Draupadi, who was rescued by Krishna. Krishna produced enough yarn from his chakra to keep her clothed. In the end, Dushyasana was exhausted and fell down on the floor, but not a patch of cloth from Draupadi's body went missing. This is said to be the turning point of Mahabharata, which led to the war between the two groups of cousins.

When they returned after their forest exile and demanded that Duryodhana (eldest of the Kauravas) give them their kingdom, the Kauravas refused. This implied war. There was no other way left for the Pandavas but to claim their throne through the means of war. Krishna played the role of the Pandavas' guide and counselor.

This is the point at which Krishna narrates the Bhagavadagita to Arjuna on the battlefield of Kurukshetra. The two warring groups were ready to lock into a battle when Arjuna developed cold feet because he was battling against his own clan or brothers. He didn't want to kill his family and thus expressed his concerns to Krishna. Krishna then played mentor and guide to him, while revealing the truth of life in the form of the Bhagavadagita that urged Arjuna to act according to his Dharma of duty. Krishna talked about how the Dharma of a warrior is to fight battles for claiming what is rightfully his without worrying about who is on the other side. Krishna urged him to follow the path of Dharma after which Arjuna fought the battle without remorse and out of a strong sense of duty towards the kingdom and its people. The battle went on for eighteen days and ended only after the Kauravas were defeated. All one hundred Kauravas perished in the battle of Kurukshetra, while the five Pandavas and Krishna lived on. The six embarked on their journey towards heaven together, but everyone except Yudhishtra died on the way. The sole Pandava reached the heavenly gates accompanied by a god who was believed to be an incarnation of Dharma. After a series of constancy, dependability, and faithfulness tests, Yudhishtra united with his brothers and wife Draupadi blissfully in heaven.

Mahabharata is an enormous epic. The Bhagavadagita is less than a percent of the entire epic of Mahabharata and is known to hold the truth about life as recited or narrated to Arjuna by Krishna on the battlefield of Kurukshetra. Bhagavadagita literally means 'song of the lord' and is also commonly referred to as 'the Gita'. The Gita finds itself in the sixth volume of the Mahabharata, just before the two warring groups embark on their battle against each other. The great warrior Arjuna pulls up his chariot in the center of the battlefield while being accompanied by his charioteer, Krishna. As discussed earlier, in a desperate fit, Arjuna threw his bow and refused to advance in the battlefield, citing the immortality of the act of war and killing his own as the reason behind his refusal to fight. In a moment of exceptionally high drama, time came to a standstill. The armies froze, and the voice of God began to speak. The situation turned grave. A mighty kingdom was on the path of self-destruction while mocking Dharma or the eternal ethical and moral laws and code of conduct that ruled the universe. Arjuna's objections and concerns weren't unfounded. He was caught in a tricky situation. On the one hand, he faced people who, as per Dharma, deserved his honor and respect. While on the other hand, as a warrior, his Dharma demanded that he kill them and lay claim to the throne. No victory fruits seemed to justify the heinous act of killing one's own people. Arjuna was caught in a dilemma that didn't seem to have any solution. It is a state of high moral and confusion that we find ourselves in throughout several situations in life. The Gita sets out to simplify this ethical or moral confusion in Arjuna's mind.

When Arjuna refused to move ahead and fight, Krishna lost his patience. However, once he realized Arjuna's true despondency, he changed his stance and began teaching the dharmic action mysteries of the universe to Arjuna. He not just introduced Arjuna to the structure and patterns of the universe, but also shared knowledge about the concepts of nature, gunas, and man's primordial nature, and took Arjuna on a journey of philosophical ideas and concepts of salvation or liberation of the soul. He talked about the significance of rituals, the Brahman principle and slowly revealed himself as the highest Almighty, much to the amazement and fear of Arjuna, who bowed before him in reverence.

Krishna allowed Arjuna to view him in his ethereal, supernal form as Vishvarupa, which ended up instilling fear in Arjuna's heart. The remaining part of the Gita intensifies and supports ideas put forth by Krishna before the ultimate epiphany. There are several ideas discussed by Krishna such as faith, unselfishness, self-control, fairness, equality, balance, and above everything else, bhakti or devotion for the Lord.

Krishna guided Arjuna about how he could go on to attain immortality by going beyond things that form primordial matter along with character, code of conduct, and behavior. Krishna emphasized the relevance of walking on the path of one's duty, declaring that it was always better to perform one's duty without differentiation rather than to doing someone else's duty well. At the end of Krishna's discourse, Arjuna was convinced to fight, true to his Dharma. In a dramatic turn of events, he picked up his bow and arrow and was ready to advance into the battlefield.

Here is some background information about the Bhagavadagita. The Gita is a conversation that occurs within a conversation. It happened when the blind father of Kauravas, Dhritarashtra, started by asking Sanjaya a question. Sanjaya (his minister as well as charioteer) relayed to him everything that was happening on the battlefield. Legend has it that since Dhritarashtra is blind, Vyasa (Dhritarashtra's father) proposed to restore his eyesight to enable him to follow events on the battlefield. Dhritarashtra refused this offer, sensing that seeing the killing of his clan and kinsmen would do him more harm than good. Instead, Vyasa bestowed powers of clairvoyance as well as clairaudience upon Sanjaya. Sanjaya came in and out throughout as he related the sequence of events to Dhritarashtra, in addition to the conversation happening between

Arjuna and Krishna. Thus, Sanjaya described the situation of Arjuna asking questions and Krishna replying to his questions.

Ganesha and Mahabharata

The Mahabharata is known to be one of the greatest epics of human civilization. Until the modern era, the two epics of Ramayana and Mahabharata were the only primary sources providing folk entertainment as well as history to people within the Indian subcontinent. They not just entertained people for long but also enlightened them about concepts such as morality, liberation, and duty. These epics often serve as the references points for rituals, ceremonies, and religious practices.

Other than spiritual value, the epic of Mahabharata also offers plenty of information about the ancient era and how denizens lived and functioned before the great flood period. The Mahabharata mentioned lineages of 24 emperors who ruled the planet at the onset of human civilization and the manner in which the epic itself originated through the enlightenment of the sage Ved Vyasa. The holy text of Hindus, Bhavadagita, comprises 700 verses segregated into eighteen chapters that form an integral component of the Mahabharata, which makes the narrative a bigger epic than a mere war tale.

There are many lessons to be learned from the Mahabharata, a story conceived by the great seer Ved Vyasa, also referred to as Krishna-Dwapayana in the form of a poem. It is believed that when Ved Vyasa started reciting the Mahabharata, it was Lord Ganesha who wrote it.

Bhagavan Vyasa, a well-known creator of the Vedas, was the offspring of the mighty sage Parasara. Ved Vyas is credited for being the compiler and creator of Mahabharata. Having compiled the Mahabharata, he decided to give the sacred tale of Dharma, valor, and familial bonds to the world. Vyasa meditated before Brahma, the creator of the universe, who revealed himself before the sage. Vyasa urged Brahma to write down the entire story while he dictated it.

Brahma then went on tell Vyasa that he should invoke Lord Ganesha who would write down his work on a leaf. Thus, sage Ved Vyasa meditated on Ganesha, who manifested before him. Vyasa welcomed him reverence and urged him to write the Mahabharata, a powerful story conceived by Vyasa.

Ganesha agreed only on the condition that he would write as long as his pen would not stop, which meant Vyasa had to dictate without pausing. However, the wise seer Vyasa guarded himself well against this condition by agreeing to it yet putting forth a counter condition. He stated that Ganesha must first understand what Vyasa dictated before writing it down. Ganesha smiled and agreed. Thus, Vyasa would occasionally compose complex stanzas, which would compel Ganesha to pause for a while before writing it. This gave the wise seer the time to compose several stanzas within his mind. Thus, the Mahabharata was written or drafted by Lord Ganesha to the dictation of Ved Vyasa. Ganesha began writing after the utterance of the holy word Aum to the narration of Ved Vyasa.

We must understand why Brahma recommended Ganesha's name for writing the Mahabharata. According to Hindu philosophy, Ganesha lives in our minds as the destroyer of fear, insecurities, and doubts. He calmly listens to all we say and hears each prayer not just addressed to him but also to other deities. He then sends these prayers to other deities in their respective spheres. Lord Ganesha also symbolizes the virtue of hearing with devotion. He is represented in the iconography as a god possessing elephant ears. Ganesha personifies mastery over literature, spiritual knowledge, and psychic learning.

The other reason why Ganesha was picked over deities for writing the Mahabharata was because that it was a battle between two warring groups of cousins, the Kauravas and Pandavas, with Lord Krishna acting as the Pandavas' guide. There was no option better than Ganesha for writing a story as replete with violence as the Mahabharata. Externally, Ganesha may appear to have a calm and serene demeanor. However, he is also known to be a warrior deity who surges ahead with his army of devotees to destroy the demons in the gods' battles against the asuras (demons).

Mahabharata talks about the inevitable suffering that originates from violence, while God himself may permit violence to occur for restoring regulation and order in the world. Ganesha is considered the leader of gods, who according to their true spirit are protectors and warriors of the universe. The Pandavas were righteous and virtuous folks and devotees of God, who walked on the path of Dharma. However, they had to gear up for a disastrous war as it was the will of God himself to protect the universe from evil, inhuman and violent people who dismissed the path of Dharma. Who better than Lord Ganesha to write the story of Mahabharata than the war leader of gods? The story of Mahabharata speaks of war as a form of duty or one's Dharma in simple, everyday language that is understood by every person.

Chapter 7: Hindu Rituals and Ceremonies

Since Hinduism is such a vast and all-encompassing religion, its rituals differ from region to region. Though the philosophy behind some ceremonies, rites, and rituals remains the same, its implementation can vary according to caste (groups and communities within the broader Hindu religion). The larger India or Hindu religious system has many common links, though, which have also influenced other religious philosophies. Here's a detailed look at some common Hindu rituals, rites, concepts, and ceremonies.

Purity

One of the most striking and conspicuous aspects of Hindu religious philosophy is the distinction between purity and impurity. It is also assumed that a person carries some level of impurity within them, which has to be eliminated or neutralized prior to performing any religious ritual or rite. Therefore, Hindus go through the process of purification by bathing or washing their hands and legs before performing religious ceremonies, rituals, or entering the temple. This is one of the most typical religious actions according to Hindu

Dharma. Similarly, a Hindu is urged as much as possible to stay away from the path of impurity, namely eating flesh, killing animals, staying connected with dead things, and so on. All these actions represent pollutions that are believed to pollute a person's body, mind, and soul. Cleansing and purification using water before performing any religious ritual or ceremony is one of the most notable aspects of Hinduism.

Within the social context, people or groups who abstain from the impure are offered greater respect. Another significant feature is the belief in the efficiency of the process of sacrifice, including Vedic sacrifice. These sacrifices include offerings conducted in a regulated manner with prior preparation of a holy space and recitation of mantras along with manipulation of some objects. It is believed that these offerings along with one's good deeds (charity and other good works) collect over a period of time and decrease the person's suffering or pain in the subsequent world.

Household Worship

The home is an important place for Hindus to practice religious rituals and perform acts of worship. The most significant times of the day for performing household religious rituals are dawn and dusk. Hindus often bathe early in the day and begin their day by lighting small oil lamps and incense sticks in the home temple before performing puja (religious rituals involving bathing the idols, garlanding them, and praying to them). The act of performing puja is believed to bring about positive energy vibrations throughout the space. Similarly, when lights come on in the evening, Hindus worship this illumination by lighting mud lamps and incense sticks. The entire household is lit up with regular lights during evening puja or worship. No room in the household is left dark. Some households sing hymns such as "shubham karoti kalyanam, arogyam, dhana sampadah, shatru buddhi vinashaya, deepa jyoti namostute", roughly translated: "let there be auspicious light, prosperity, and wealth in our household. Let our evil mind be defeated. We pray to the flame of light to bestow its blessings upon us." This is a typical evening prayer. Some households will also leave their main entrance doors open during the evening rituals because it is widely believed that this is when Goddess Lakshmi or the goddess of wealth walks into the house. The door is left open to welcome her. Darkness and sleeping during the time of evening worship are believed to be inauspicious. Family members are expected to take a bath or wash their hands and feet entering the household puja room or space, which is considered to be the most sacred space in a Hindu home. Many households do not allow people to walk into the puja room or space wearing their footwear. Though there are two main important times of worship (dawn and dusk) in Hindu religion, many devout families engage in greater acts of devotion throughout the day.

Typically, in villages and small towns, and even in more devout city homes, Hindu women begin their day by drawing auspicious geometric patterns (called rangoli in Hindu tradition) using chalk powder or rice flour on their doorstep or at the entrance of the house. This is especially popular during festivals such as Diwali. Adults, as well as children, are encouraged to sing hymns, recite mantras (such as the Gayatri mantra), and pray to the Sun God in the morning. A lot of Hindus practice Surya Namaskar or yogic kriya (a series of postures performed in a sequence to show reverence to the Sun God early in the morning) facing the sun. This is believed not to just offer tons of fitness benefits but also purify the body, mind, and soul before you begin the day. Here is the complete Gayatri mantra, which can be chanted during puja at dawn or/and dusk: "Aum bhur bhuvasvaha, tatsavitur varenyam, bhargo devasya deemahi, diyoyona prachodaya, aum." Several other Sanskrit prayers and chants are also recited during puja or other religious rituals/ceremonies.

Puja or worship of the goddess and gods comprises a variety of daily rituals in Hinduism. It can be a combination of offerings, prayers, and other rituals depending on the community, caste, region, and individual household practices. Typically, Hindus households will either perform puja daily (twice a day) or during auspicious days and festivals. The puja is performed before the idol or a deity or a sacred religious symbol or holy guru (such as Sai Baba). In its more advanced forms, puja or worship comprises a sequence of rituals starting from personal purification, invocation of gods, and offerings of food, flowers, garlands, and other items, such as clothing or pieces of cloth, accompanied by prayers.

While some devoted worshippers perform puja in their household daily, others move from one temple to another for the purpose of performing puja. In the temple, puja is performed by oneself or with the help of the temple priest. These priests accept offerings from devotees and present the offerings to God on behalf of the devotees. These offerings are kept before the idols, and some part of them (especially the foodstuff) is given back to the devotee as Prashad or holy food. The gifts become sacred once they come into contact with the idols and images of Hindu gods and goddesses, which is why they are received with absolute reverence with the right hand (considered the pure hand for performing most auspicious religious rituals) as divine grace.

Sacred ash along with other items (such as saffron powder) is often distributed to everyone in the household or temple after performing puja. It is mostly smeared on the forehead (known to be the center of the Third Eye in Hinduism, an energy center responsible for knowledge, psychic abilities, intuition, and wisdom) by the priest or household member who has conducted the puja. In modern Hindu homes, puja is not as much of a long-winded process. It may simply comprise of people getting together, holding hands before idols or images of gods and goddesses, and saying a small prayer before going about their daily tasks. A simple prayer may be offered to a divine image. It isn't uncommon for Hindus throughout India to stop before a place of worship or temple when they are traveling and fold their hands in reverence. You'll often find people who are passing by temples stop for a while and pray for divine intervention or offer a brief invocation to God.

Post bathing (an important form of purification), Hindu families bathe their gods and goddesses in gangajal or holy water from the Ganges. Gods in the shrine are wiped clean after which a lamp is lit to illuminate the small home temple. Foodstuff (mostly sweets) is also offered to gods by placing it before the idols. This is later consumed by members of the household and guests as Prashad or holy food. Prayers are usually recited in Sanskrit or other religious dialects, depending upon the community of people and region they inhabit. In the evening, especially in small towns and villages, womenfolk gather in a temple or house to sing bhajans or hymns praising God. This is followed by the distribution of Prashad or holy food.

In more religious or orthodox Hindu homes, some food is set aside during every meal to be donated to the homeless or beggars. Small amounts of grains are also offered to animals and birds according to the guidance of certain priests or religious leaders to attract merit for the clan, please ancestors, or cleanse karma dosh (karmic debt or fault). Hindus believe in accumulating good karma for the family through acts of self-sacrifice. You will often find devout Hindus releasing a few drops of water onto their dinner plate to cleanse the meal before offering a prayer, after which they will begin eating. This prayer is offered to Annapurna or the goddess of food, though modern Hindus will say a general 'thank you for the meal' prayer.

Pregnancy and Birth

Hindus perform ceremonies during the pregnancy stage to pray for the health and well-being of the mother and soon to be born child. The child's father parts the mother's hair thrice upward from front to back to ensure growth and development of the tiny embryo. At times, charms are also utilized for warding off the evil. Before a child's umbilical cord is cut, the father touches the little one's lips with a golden spoon dipped in honey or clarified butter (ghee), while "vak" (meaning speech) is whispered into the baby's right ear thrice. This can be followed by chanting a series of mantras for the baby's prosperity, good health, and long life.

There are a number of rituals involving the infant, including its first visit to the temple, first solid food feeding (the infant is usually given cooked rice in a ceremony known as Annaprashan), ear piercing, and haircutting (known as 'mundan', which is usually performed in a temple where the hair is offered to the deity).

Upanayana (thread ceremony)

The upanayana or thread ceremony is known to be one of the most sacred ceremonies in the lifespan of upper caste Hindus. It is an initiation ceremony that is conducted for young Hindu males between the ages of six and twelve, marking the transformation of childhood to awareness of adult religious obligations. Typically, a family priest will put a sacred thread on the boy's left shoulder (it has to be worn forever), while the parents guide the boy to recite the Gayatri Mantra while the thread is being invested. This initiation ceremony is viewed as renewed birth, which makes the person who is wearing it entitled to be referred to as "twice-born".

In the earlier categorization of Hindu society into four main castes (with plenty of sub-castes within the complex caste structure), only the three higher castes or Brahmins (religious priests), Kshatriyas (warriors), and Vaishyas (merchants and traders) were permitted to wear this sacred thread. This was to identify them from the fourth caste or groups of menial workers (Shudras). Hindu women in Southern India undergo another ritual or celebration when they get their first menses.

Hindu Weddings

Weddings are another important transition in a Hindu's life when a person moves from the Brahmacharya or celibacy stage towards Kama (or fulfilling pro-recreational responsibilities). In a majority of Hindu weddings, an auspicious date and time for the wedding are pre-decided by the elders of a household in consultation with the family astrologer or priest. The wedding rituals happen only at a pre-determined auspicious time.

At a typical Hindu wedding, the bride and groom symbolize a god and goddess. According to tradition, the groom represents a prince who comes to wed and take away his princess. This is why the groom is decked in bright finery and made to ride over a white mare accompanied by a fervent procession taken out by the groom's family (known as baraat). The process comprises, among other things, the groom's relatives, a band of musicians, and opulent electrified lamps.

Before the wedding, the bride and her family celebrate the application of henna on her hand and feet, which can take hours. The Mehendi ceremony is usually celebrated a day or two prior to the actual wedding ceremony. The groom's name is usually written on the bride's hand with henna by the henna artist. The ceremony is marked by plenty of singing, rendition of dhols (and other musical instruments) and dancing by women relatives of the bride, praising or playfully teasing her to mark the occasion of the auspicious henna filling her hands.

Hindu wedding ceremonies are often elaborate and consist of a series of rituals based on caste, communities, and regions. Typically, there is a priest helming the ceremony who chants mantras for the happiness and well-being of the couple, while they exchange garlands and take seven rounds northwards around the holy fire (known as saat pheras or seven rounds), while also making offerings into the fire. Each of the rounds represents a promise or commitment the bride and groom make for the success and well-being of their marriage. Seven is one of the holiest numbers of Hindu religion, and as such, the seven pheras represent a union that is believed to last for seven lifetimes. This means that the bride and groom promise to stay together not just in this lifetime but also in the next seven lifetimes. Hindus perceive marriage as a sacrosanct bond and not a contract, unlike more modern societies. To signify the union, a fire is lit and said to be a witness of the holy union of the man and woman. Offerings are made in the fire by both the bride and groom while praying for their happy union.

The bride's brother hands over three handfuls of puffed rice to her as a good wish for a lifetime of happiness. Every time, the bride puts the rice into the holy fire.

One of the many ceremonies or rituals of a Hindu wedding is the Jai Mala, where the bride and groom exchange flower garlands. This expresses their desire to spend the rest of the lifetime (and the next seven lifetimes) together. In western countries, the Hindu bride and groom may also exchange rings.

Another ceremony that is typically followed in Hindu weddings is kanyadaan, where the bride's father places his daughter's hands on the hands of the groom, symbolizing giving her away to the groom. It is a gesture where the father hands over his daughter to the groom and urges him to take good care of her. At times, the father pours water over the bride's hands which also trickle through her fingers into the groom's hands signifying a union of the two for several lifetimes.

The bride and groom's clothes are tied together as they go around the sacred ceremonial fire. Every round represents a commitment they make to each other or a blessing they seek from the gods. The main objective of the saat pheras or saptapadi is establishing a friendship between the bride and groom, which is believed to be one of the most important aspects of the union. In olden times, and even today in Indian villages and small towns, the bride and groom's match is often fixed by elders in the family. This means they do not even see each other until the time of getting married. The saat pheras are therefore believed to be a symbol for them establishing a union based on friendship for living together throughout several lifetimes.

Another typical Hindu marriage ritual involves the application of red powder or sindoor to the bride (just above the forehead or parting of the hair) by the groom. The red powder symbolizes good luck and fertility and is typically applied by married women in India. Since red symbolizes prosperity, fertility, good luck, and the rising sun, the bride often dons a red attire during the wedding ceremony.

The groom puts a necklace of gold and black beads around the bride's neck, which is known as the mangalsutra. Along with the sindoor, this is often worn by married women in India for good health, prosperity, and well-being of their union. Traditionally, it is believed that Lakshmi, the Hindu goddess of good fortune, prosperity, and wealth, is invoked on wearing the mangalsutra, and therefore, the bride receives divine blessings from the goddess throughout her married life.

Hastamilap is where the bride's and groom's hands are placed over one another. Generally, the bride places her right hand on the groom's right hand. Their right hands are thereafter tied together using a cotton thread by winding it around several times. The priest continues to chant holy verses and mantras as the couple's tied hands symbolize the union of several lifetimes. Why is the thread tied so many times around their hands? It is a deep metaphor for an unbreakable bond. While a single thread can be broken easily, a thread that is wound several times around the hands of the couple cannot be easily broken, thus representing an unbreakable bond.

Before beginning the wedding ceremony (or any ceremony for that matter), Hindus begin with an invocation to Lord Ganesha, the elephant god who is known to be the remover of obstacles (which is why he is also referred to as Vignaharta or he who gains victory over obstacles) and harbinger of wisdom, good fortune, and salvation. It is considered highly auspicious to take his name before beginning any ceremony. The Ganesh pooja is typically performed a few days before the actual wedding ceremony.

There can be a variation of these rituals based on different castes and regions.

Death and Funerals

After a family member passes away, the relatives participate in several ceremonies, beginning with the preparation of the dead body for the funeral procession to the crematorium. A majority of Hindus cremate the deceased instead of practicing burial. There are also a few groups who practice burial but by and large cremation is the preferred funeral method of the Hindus. At the funeral site or crematorium, in the presence of several male relatives and mourners (women are usually not allowed to enter the future site or crematorium), the deceased's closest relative (generally the oldest son) precedes over the last rites by lighting the funeral pyre. The relatives and mourners are generally dressed in white and other somber colors to symbolize grieving.

Once cremation is done, the ashes and bone fragments (known as asthi) of the deceased are accumulated in an earthen pot and released into the holy river. Every person who participates in funeral takes a purifying bath once the rituals are over. The family of the deceased remains in a state of pollution for a particular number of days (ten or thirteen), which they invite Brahmin priests and other relatives for a ceremonial meal. Gifts are given to the less fortunate while seeking their blessings for the soul of the deceased. During memorial service, panda or rice balls are given to the spirit or soul of the deceased. These ceremonies are not just believed to contribute to the overall good deeds of the deceased but also for the pacification of their soul so that it doesn't linger around as a spirit and passes through the Yama, the Hindu god of death.

Bathing in Holy Rivers

Every river that flows in India is revered and believed to be sacred. They are believed to be purifiers since they are closely linked with a Hindu deity or saint. Rivers play an important role in Hinduism owing to the belief that they help people get rid of their sins, evils, and impurities by bathing in the holy water of these rivers. Rivers are also considered a way to make offerings to God. Since ancient times, when nature was worshipped as a god or the forces of god, rivers have been considered the source of life. In ancient civilizations, every aspect of the civilization was centered on significant rivers. Think about ancient eastern civilizations such as the city of Mohenjo-daro that came into being around Harappa River.

Hence, rivers play an important part in purification rituals and devotional worship. Several Hindu temples are located on the river banks of Ganga, Narmada, Krishna, Godavari, Yamuna, and others on auspicious occasions for the elimination of sins and salvation. Of all Indian rivers, Ganga is considered the most sacred, purest, and auspicious by Hindus. Hindus strive to bathe in the Holy Ganges at least once on their lifetime to wash away their sins. Merely dipping themselves in the Holy Ganges is believed to cleanse one's sins and set them on the path of liberation. The Kumbh Mela Festival, which is celebrated once every twelve years at each of India's four sacred rivers, is considered extremely auspicious.

Dana or Charity

Dana or gift giving is integral to the Dharma of Hinduism along with the rituals, spiritualism, and practices. Vedic sacrifices are known to facilitate charity, giving, and gifting. It is the obligatory Dharma of higher caste Hindus to undertake acts of sacrifices five times a day while making offerings of food and other items to sages, other creatures, ancestors, gods, and less privileged humans. In Vedic sacrifices, worshippers offer food to gods, seers, and guests. Gifts are also offered to priests officiating these ceremonies.

Vedas and holy books encourage offering gifts to priests or Brahmans, as they are known in Sanskrit. They are known to selflessly devote their lives to upholding Dharma and guide people in upholding Dharma. In Hinduism, Brahmans are known to restore order, balance, and regularity in humans, while strengthening their connection with God. The Manusmiriti (holy Hindu scripture or text) suggests that it is obligatory for Vaishyas (traders) and Kshatriyas (warriors) to make sacrifices and offer gifts to deserving people and that a gift offered to an ignorant person offers no reward. The timing of offering gifts is vital. For instance, it is believed that a student or shisha should not offer any gift to his teacher or guru until he/she completes his/her education.

71

What gifts of charity are approved or ascribed by Hinduism? Some gifts that are typically approved for charity in Hinduism are food, gold, land, wealth for construction of a water tank or tank, and cattle. When there is dosha or fault in one's kundali or stars, priests and/or astrologers will often advise Hindus to correct this dosha or karmic/astro faults by performing acts of charity, such as feeding cows, dogs, or birds on a particular day of the week. Similarly, other fire sacrifices and pujas may be suggested for pleasing angered forces or God.

Vratas and Pilgrimages

Vratas are fasts or abstinence from food and water that is recommended in Hindu law books or Hinduism for overcoming one's sin, cleansing the body, and attaining purification of the soul. Fasts may be performed throughout the year (one a particular day of the week) or as part of certain festivals (such as Navratri), rituals, and sacrificial ceremonies. Manusmiriti describes Vratas as a way of eliminating one's sins that arise as a result of offenses such as shedding the blood of the holy beings or Brahmans.

Although fasting is primarily practiced by women in India, both women and men may perform it to fulfill their wishes, seek divine blessings of the Almighty, and prove their devotion and allegiance to a particular deity. The vrata or fasting is seen as a form of penance, a punishment or ritual of purification to eliminate the consequences of bad karma, adversity, and impurities. The fast may last for a day or many days or months at a time. During this period, devotees are expected to perform vows and stick to a strict code of conduct.

Fasting can be for the entire duration of the fast or via consuming specific meals during specific times. All the same, the devotees' minds are also spiritually charged, where they engage in spiritual thoughts, read scriptures, hear religious discourses, practice righteous conduct, engage in worship, undertake celibacy, practice truthfulness, and several other virtues.

Visiting places of pilgrimages is considered the Dharma of a true Hindu. The Indian subcontinent is filled with innumerable sacred places, rivers, mountains, and more. These forces of nature have forever been associated with sages, sacred events, forms, gods, and incarnations, and more, which are believed to possess the power to clean and purify the sins while granting either a comfortable or good life or salvation.

In Hinduism, making a pilgrimage is considered to be a form of self-cleansing, expressing gratitude, showing devotion, and pledging commitment to Dharma. The Puranas suggest that pilgrimages to holy places or tirthas offer devotees several opportunities for atoning their sins, seeking forgiveness, and experiencing peace, joy, and happiness. Popular pilgrimage spots, such as Gaya, Dwarka, Kashi, Prayaga, and others, are known to hold special spiritual powers that cleanse devotees who visit them and instill a sense of spiritual power in them to embark on a more virtuous path of liberation.

One suggested way of neutralizing sinful karma is by accumulating positive or virtuous karma, although this is not considered the ideal resolution for the karmic problem. Visiting holy places, engaging in acts of devotion, and making sacrifices are known to be several ways for balancing one's karma.

The Bhagavadagita suggests that a person should perform actions without the desire or attachment for the results of these actions. They should be practiced as a sacrifice for God rather than appeasing oneself or with the intention of selfishly correcting one's karma. You cannot go on a rampage of collecting bad karma and think it can be corrected by performing some acts of sacrifices or going on a pilgrimage. The intention behind an action is as important as the action itself. Lord Krishna himself has stated that (and the quote has been widely misused by people to justify their evil actions), "a lie that brings some good is equivalent to a hundred truths." Thus, it isn't just the action but also the intention behind the action that counts or holds relevance.

The Bhagavadagita states that a person should perform the right actions with the right intentions without focusing on the benefits or advantages of these actions. Virtue is important for cleansing karma. In Hinduism, a traditional purification method for cleansing the body, mind, and spirit is practicing virtue and adhering to the path of Dharma. Along with fasting, going on a pilgrimage, and undertaking acts of sacrifice, abiding by an ethical code of conduct should not be overlooked when it comes to cleansing one's spirit or balancing karma. Hindu scriptures suggest that attributes like non-violence, non-stealing, contentment, and truthfulness are considered purifying. These practices lead to the collection of meritorious or good karma along with eliminating negative karma from one's past life.

Hindu Symbols and Their Relevance

Being one of the oldest religions in the world, Hinduism features more symbols, images, and iconography than any other religion in the world. Some religious scholars are of the opinion that no other major world religion employs art and symbolism as efficiently as Hinduism. A majority of symbols used in Hinduism represent philosophies, learnings from scriptures, and deities. There are two main categories of Hindu symbols – the hand gestures and body positioning (known as mudras) and illustrations and icons (known as murtis).

Here are some of the most common Hindu symbols and a brief explanation of their relevance:

Om (also known as aum)

The Om is the most powerful and universal Hindu symbol. Its sound vibration is known to contain the vibration of the entire universe, which is why it is extensively used during meditation. Om is the foremost syllable of every Hindu prayer. Moreover, it is utilized as a symbol of the universe and the highest reality. Some people are of the opinion that Om represents God's three fundamental aspects – Brahma (the creator), Vishnu (the sustainer), and Shiva (the destroyer). You'll find several Hindus wearing Om lockets, rings, T-shirts, and other similar items.

The Swastika

Although in some regions of the world the Swastika has negative connotations (thanks to Hitler's Nazi regime), in Hinduism, it is essentially a sign of good luck, prosperity, and well-being. You'll often find swastikas on the main entrance doors of Hindu households. They are also drawn outside Hindu homes as rangolis during pujas, festivals, and other special occasions. If you observe closely, the swastika is nothing but a variation of a cross. It has been in existence since ancient Hinduism and is believed to represent, among other things, truth, goodness, honesty, stability, integrity, and purity. It is one of the most auspicious symbols of Hinduism and is drawn on doors of new homes before the owners/occupants of the property step into them. The four angles and points of the swastika present the four directions (north, south, east, and west) or the four Vedas (Rigveda, Yajurveda, Samaveda, and Atharvaveda). There are several other interesting religious and geometrical attributes and aspects to the swastika, which have found their way in popular works of fiction such as Dan Brown's *The Da Vinci Code.*

The Tilaka

The tilaka is a semi-circle on top of an inverted triangular like symbol that is often spotted in the foreheads of devout Hindus. Traditionally, Hindus applied a tilaka of sandalwood while performing their post-bath, morning puja rituals. A symbol in the middle of the forehead is also worn by Hindu women in the form of bindis (which can be simple as well as decorative). This region above the nose and between the two eyebrows is known to be a very powerful energy center that houses the Third Eye. When activated, the Third Eye is known to offer inexhaustible reserves of wisdom, knowledge, and psychic powers to the individual. The tilaka is believed to represent the Third Eye and hence stands for wisdom and spiritual awakening. Thus, it is often spotted on the foreheads of religious and spiritually inclined Hindus.

Though it is typically semi-circular or triangular, the tilaka comes in several shapes and forms depending on the religious ritual or ceremony. A 'U' shaped tilaka typically represents devotion to Lord Vishnu, while three horizontal lines depict devotion for Lord Shiva.

Rudraksha

The Rudraksha is a tree that grows mostly in Southeast Asia, the Himalayas, Australia, and Nepal. The most fascinating aspect about this tree is that its seeds are believed to represent the tears of Shiva, the destroyer of the universe. According to an ancient Hindu legend, when Shiva witnessed the suffering of his people, a tear slowly shed from his eye, which eventually grew into the Rudraksha tree. The name of the tree comes from "Rudra" (another name of Lord Shiva) and "aksha", which translates to mean "eyes." The seeds of this tree are believed to be holy and are often worn on the necks and wrists of devout Hindus for their positive vibrations and properties. Prayer beads and rosaries are also created out of Rudraksha.

Shiva Lingam

Several deities represent natural forces in Hinduism. These are wind (Vayu), earth (Prithvi), Agni (fire), and sun (Surya). There are many icons used for representing these natural element deities. The Shiva lingam is known to represent the force and power of the procreator. It is an elongated cylindrical structure that resembles an erect penis.

Trishula

The trishula or trident is one of the most prominent and widely recognized symbols of Hinduism, which is closely associated with Lord Shiva. It is a three-pronged pointed weapon like element that is believed to be Lord Shiva's weapon of protection, preservation, and restoration. Hindus believe Lord Shiva uses the trishula for ensuring balance and dharma in the universe, though there are several other deeper and esoteric meanings to the symbol. It also represents the trinity of Brahma, Vishnu, and Mahesh, and stands as a symbol of the forces of preservation, creation, and destruction. It is also known as symbolizing the three gunas – Sattvam, Rajas, and Tamas. Another important symbolic representation of the holy trishula is the three attributes or realms of consciousness – conation, cognition, and affection.

Sri Yantra

The Sri Yantra is known to be one of the holiest Hindu symbols. It is also referred to as the Sri Chakra in some parts of the Indian subcontinent. The symbol comprises of nine triangles that are interlocked and originate from a main, central point. Out of the nine triangles, four upward facing triangles represent the masculine aspect of Lord Shiva, while the five downward facing triangles represent the feminine aspect of Lord Shiva or Shakti, as it's referred to (also divine mother). On the whole, Sri Yantra is utilized for representing the union of the universe's masculine and feminine energies or masculine or feminine divinity. On the whole, it signifies the bond of all elements in the cosmos. References to the Sri Yantra have found themselves in several religious texts, works of art, and other Hindu works.

Hindu Festivals

Diwali or Deepavali

Diwali is one of the most important and popular Hindu festivals celebrated in India and throughout the world. It is celebrated during the auspicious Hindu month of Ashwayuja or Ashwin (October or November) as per the Hindu lunar calendar depending on the movement and positions of the sun and moon.

Deepavali in Sanskrit literally translates into "row of lights". Though its origins are not known, it is believed to commemorate the occasion of Lord Rama returning from exile with his wife, Sita, and brother, Lakshamana. The people of Ayodhya welcomed their beloved king by lighting the streets with oil lamps, a symbol of happiness, prosperity, and awakening. Then there are references to it being celebrated as a harvest festival in India.

Vedic people were of the view that dead souls who weren't destined for salvation made their way into the ancestral real, which was housed on the moon through the ancestors' path or pitrmarg. The path was not well illuminated as the sun-soaked path of the immortals, so people were believed to have flashed lamps, lights, and bright torches in the direction of the sky hoping that will help the embark on a journey into the ancestral world.

There are references to Diwali or the festival of lights in the ancient Puranas. According to the Skanda Purana, lamps that were brightly lit on that specific day represented attributes of the sun. Diwali is connected with many ancient legends like the rise of Nachiketa to heaven, the triumph of Lord Rama over Ravana and his subsequent return to the kingdom of Ayodhya after fourteen years in exile, the Pandavas returning from exile to stake their claim to the throne of Hastinapura, and the victory of Krishna over the demon Narakasura.

In some Indian states, people believe that Bali (the demon king who was offered salvation by Vishnu) visited the planet to witness people celebrating Diwali with pomp and grandeur. Hindus also strongly believe that the goddess Lakshmi (the goddess of wealth) enters their homes during Diwali Laxmi Pujan and blesses them with wealth and prosperity. This is why merchants and households worship her on the day of Laxmi Pujan and keep their homes squeaky clean during Diwali. It is believed that she enters only clean and well-kept homes, which is why plenty of Hindus spring clean their homes just before Diwali. Even outside India, Diwali is widely celebrated by the Indians across the world as part of community celebrations.

While the exact antecedents of one of the most popular Hindu festivals remain unknown, goddess Lakshmi (known as Lakme in French) is said to be the main presiding goddess of the festival of lights. Goddess Lakshmi represents all the universe's positive forces, such as wealth, good fortune, fertility, beauty, victory, happiness, health, courage, and abundance. The festival is marked as a celebration of wealth and during the auspicious time of Lakshmi Pujan (often on the second or third day of Deepawali in the evenings), Hindus worship their wealth by keeping coins and bills in their home temple and singing in hymns in praise of the goddess of wealth (aum jai Lakshmi mata). Much like the goddess Lakshmi herself, Diwali symbolizes the abundance, illumination, and brilliance of life in its fullest glory.

Several Hindus celebrate or mark the onset of a new year on the second or third day of Diwali known as 'padava'. Historically, padava marked the onset of a new accounting period for businessmen. As the name implies, Diwali is celebrated as a festival of sounds, lights, and joyful festivities. Hindus consider Diwali as a good opportunity to begin new relationships, renew hopes, and start new ventures. The festival represents values of brotherhood, love, sharing, illumination/enlightenment, and more.

Hindu households typically begin the first day of Diwali by bathing in the early hours of the morning, followed by drawing rangoli patterns and auspicious symbols at their doorstep. Before bathing, Hindus apply 'ubtan' or paste made of natural ingredients on their bodies and faces to lend it a festival glow. It is also seen as a form of purification. Women often prepare sweets and savories, which are shared with family members, friends, and neighbors. Once day melts into night, one can observe brightly lit homes, skies, and streets everywhere. The brilliance of lamps, lanterns, and firecrackers illuminates every space. Public places throughout India and other parts of the world are crowded with adults and children burning firecrackers after evening puja. It is symbolic of the mortal beings on Earth expressing their rejection of evil, while wholeheartedly embracing their commitment to walking on the path of Dharma, duty, morality, and devotion. Lights spell divinity and Hindus reinforce their belief and commitment towards the divine by lighting up their homes and street on the occasion of Diwali.

The first day of Diwali is known as Dhanteras or Choti Diwali (small Diwali). Dhan translates into wealth and Dhanteras is celebrated on the thirteenth day of the initial half of the lunar month. Legend has it that Lord Dhanwantri emerged from the ocean waters holding wisdom about the Ayurvedic medicines to help humankind battle sickness and death. People purchase valuables, new clothes, and utensils since it is considered auspicious to buy new things on this day. People light earthen lamps outside their houses to welcome illumination, wealth, prosperity, and good fortune into their homes.

The second day of the festival is known as Naraka Chaturdashi, meaning hell and fourteenth day since the day falls on the fourteenth day of the initial half of the lunar month. The day signifies the end of an era of evil in prehistoric times and the advent of a new era of wisdom, illumination, knowledge, and learning. Legend has it that on the day of Narak Chaturdashi, Lord Krishna, accompanied by Satyabhama and his large army, slew the Narkasura demon in a battle between the devas and asuras (or gods and demons) to free the world from the shadows of oppression, ignorance, darkness, inequality, and fear. During this process, Lord Krishna is also believed to have released 16,000 divine energies of goddesses, which were trapped by evil demonic forces. Hindus take a ritual bath using herbs just like Lord Krishna did after returning victorious from the battle. On this day, while bathing, Hindus crush a traditional fruit to symbolize crushing or killing the demons or rakshasa. Post bathing, they light diyas outside the house, perform puja, draw rangolis at the doorstep, and light a few crackers as a symbol of good luck and prosperity.

Holi

Holi is another significant festival celebrated during spring in the Indian subcontinent (mainly India and Nepal) and across the world by the Indian community. It is also called "the festival of colors" since playing with color powder is an important aspect of the festival. It also has several other regional names as per different communities, languages, and regions throughout India.

The festival of Holi comes on the Phalguna full moon day, usually during March – since the date varies each year according to the Hindu lunar calendar. Holi represents the triumph of good over bad. It also symbolizes the onset of spring season. For people, this is an occasion to get together for merriment, express thankfulness for a wonderful harvest, and mend broken relationships. Holi is also believed to be the festival of forgiveness meant to create harmony between people. Conventionally, this is the day to let go of old enmities and start relationships on a new note.

In India, Holi typically begins with Holika Dahan that symbolizes the burning of Holika, the demoness. A night before rang panchami (color play), people gather on open ground to sing, dance, and pray around a huge bonfire. They circle around the fire, offering prayers or singing songs. This is followed by applying gulal (traditional red colored powder) on each other's cheeks while offering festival wishes and greetings to each other.

The next day is Holi Rangapanchami, where people gather outside their homes or public places to celebrate and play with colors. There are mock water jet and water balloon fights in some parts of India, especially among the youngsters. Powder-infused colored water and dry color powders are extensively used during the merriment and celebrations. People use water guns as well as buckets of colored or dirty water on each other. The cheer and loud merry-making voices are punctuated by sounds of drums and other musical instruments that are carried out by people during processions. Holi is typically celebrated by people visiting each other, playing with colors, dancing, and consuming sweets mixed with bhang (an intoxicant extracted from cannabis leaves).

Holi comes from the word Holika. Legend has it that Holika, the demoness, was the sister of the demon king Hiranyakasipu (who owing to a boon of invincibility from the gods became intolerant and wicked). His son, Prahlad, was a devout follower of Vishnu, which angered Hiranyakasipu. To discourage and prevent his son from worshipping Vishnu, the demon subjected him to excessive physical torture. Prahlad didn't relent. Finally, the sister of the demon, Holika, decided to step in to help Hiranyakasipu. She decided to trick little Prahlad into sitting with her on a burning pyre while she wore a magic cloak that would make her immune to burning, injury, or destruction. Prahlad wasn't given any protective gear and was absolutely vulnerable. As Holika sat on the pyre with her nephew Prahlad on her lap, the fire became intense. The cloak is believed to have flown from her being and onto the body of young Prahlad. This resulted in Prahlad being saved while his evil aunt brunt to ashes. Legend has it that later Vishnu manifested himself as Narasimha (half-man half-lion) from a pillar in Hiranyakasipu's palace and slayed the demon.

People are said to celebrate the occasion of Holi by setting bonfires to represent the triumph of good over evil and the destruction of the demoness or negative forces outside as well as within them. In earlier times, once the fire subsided, people applied its ashes on each other's foreheads. However, over time, ashes were replaced with colors.

Navratri

Navratri literally translates into nine nights. It is another important festival in the Hindu calendar, which is celebrated with considerable pomp and grandeur throughout different parts of India and the world. For each of the nine days, devotees recite verses from the Ramcharitramanas by Tulsidas or watch plays (traditionally known as Ramlila or the story/song of Ram) that demonstrate incidents that occurred in the life of Lord Rama.

After celebrating Navratri for nine days, people celebrate Vijayadashami on the tenth day, where effigies of the demon king Ravana are burnt amidst plenty of fanfare to symbolize the victory of good over evil.

In eastern regions of India (Bengal), people celebrate the nine days as Durga Puja, which is why the festival is believed to be celebrated for nine days. Durga is believed to have nine forms, and for each of the nine days, a new form is believed to manifest itself. In southern India, the goddess Saraswati (the goddess of learning) is widely worshipped during Navratri. Though Navratri celebration differs from region to region in the Indian continent, the underlying theme remains that it is the festival of celebrating the goddess or female form. In the western Indian state of Gujarat, people do the garba and dandiya dance amidst loud music and catchy beats for nine nights by getting together in a large ground or public place in the brightest traditional finery and ornaments.

'Kanya Bhojan' is also an important ritual of the festival that is practiced during the eight-day (Ashtami) or ninth day (Navami) of the festival. Hindus consider this an important ritual to celebrate the goddess. During the puja, young girls (who aren't yet on their menses) are invited to households to be worshipped and fed. The girls' hands and feet are washed with water by the lady of the house. This is followed by the ladies offering prayers to the girls and touching their feet. Once the rituals are complete, the girls are served meals and given some gifts or money. The girls are known as "kanya" or virgins. You will often spot groups of young girls moving from one house to another on the day of Ashtami and Navami in India.

According to Hindu tradition, there are five distinct Navratris that are celebrated during various times of the year. On every occasion, a distinct aspect of the mighty goddess is celebrated and worshipped. The most important of these five Navratris is Sharad Navratri, which is celebrated during the month of September or October based on the Hindu lunar calendar. On the first day of Sharad Navratri, the invocation of the goddess takes place, and a clay idol of the goddess is worshipped. On the tenth or last day of the festival (Vijayadashami), the idol is carried through a grand procession on the streets and immersed in the ocean, canal, or lake. One of the most important rituals of this Navratri is fasting. People fast for nine days for the purpose of self-purification through abstinence. Devotees of the goddess also stay away from consuming liquor and meat. People across India stick to a predominantly vegetarian diet as a mark of respect for the goddess.

One question that arises when it comes to Hindu festivals is: why is the same festival celebrated differently in different parts of India? For instance, celebrations for a festival like Navratri vary vastly from east to west India. People in different parts of the country worship different deities and associate different gods/goddess with each festival. The exact origins of this or past occurrences that led to this phenomenon aren't known. However, it is believed that during prehistoric times, the festival of nine nights may have been closely associated with cults of fertility in the Indian subcontinent. Over a period of time, the philosophy of these fertility cults may have been adapted into local legends and mythology to bring on new practices. Every region may have its own variations based on the local culture, weather, needs, and points of relevance.

Celebrating Navratri is believed to be a form of pleasing the goddess through devotional worship. Invoking lady luck or goddess luck is believed to bring the devotee not only materials but also a resolution to their problems, pain, and suffering. Spiritually, the goddess is known to carry away all your impurities, demonic qualities and sins, and facilitate spiritual transformation. She is known to purify the soul and awaken one's consciousness to help a person accomplish their fullest potential. According to Hinduism, one of life's biggest challenges is overcoming an inner animal that holds us back from realizing the truth about ourselves. The inner animal is responsible for our attachments, illusions, bondage, and desires. Invoking the goddess helps you fight the inner animal or asura and bestows you with compassion, equality, and wisdom, which helps you move through the nine pathways of consciousness into the highest plane of heaven.

Ganesh Chaturthi

Ganesh Chaturthi, also known as Vinayaka Chaturthi, is celebrated to worship and honor Lord Ganesha, considered the god of all gods in Hinduism. He also goes by the name of Vigneshwara, Ganapathi, Varadha, and several other names. Ganesha is the son of Lord Shiva and the army general or leader of Shiva's warrior band known as the ganas. The festival is celebrated in the first half of the Hindu Bhadrapada month (fourth day of the month precisely), which is somewhere in the month of August and September. The date varies every year according to the Hindu lunar calendar. Hindus throughout the Indian subcontinent and abroad celebrate Ganesh Chaturthi with plenty of pomp and grandeur.

The exact tradition of how Ganesha came to be worshipped publically or when Ganesh Chaturthi first began isn't known. Ganesha didn't find mention as a Vedic deity, though there are plenty of parallels between him and popular Vedic deity Brahmanaspati, known as the guru or teacher of all Vedic gods.

The tradition of worshipping a god with the head of an elephant may have originated during the time of the royal armies, where elephants were extensively used on the battlefield as enemy destroyers. Ganesha is also known as 'Vignahartha', meaning destroyer of obstacles or evil, which means there are some parallels between the role fulfilled by elephants in the royal armies and Lord Ganesha. Irrespective of his antecedents, the fact remains that Ganesha is one of the most popular deities of India (and in fact symbolizes India in several images throughout the world). By the medieval era, Ganesha had gained popularity as a deity.

Ganesh Chaturthi wasn't always celebrated on the grand public scale that it is celebrated in today. Earlier, Ganesha was worshipped at home after the onset of the harvest season. For devotees, it was an opportunity to seek the blessings, help, and protection of the deity. These devotees expressed gratitude for the good fortune and blessings he had bestowed in their lives. Over time, though, the festival came to acquire more social and communal significance. Though people still pray to Ganesha at home, nowadays it has become an elaborate public festival. Large tents or pandals are set up in different parts of the country, where devotees visit in large numbers to seek blessings from huge Ganesha idols (there is often a competition between different groups or pandals about whose idols, sets, and decorations are the best). Devotees often move from one pandal to another (and, at times, wait in a queue outside the pandal or tent for several hours) to catch a glimpse of Ganesha and seek his divine blessings. There are musical performances, orchestras, entertainment programs, and competitions in public places to mark the occasion of Ganesh Chaturthi.

Ganesh Chaturthi is a ten-day festival that begins on the first day (or day of Ganesha Chaturthi) with 'mukhsdarsha', where the elephant-headed god's face is unveiled, and puja is performed to invoke him. People gather around the idol in their homes or public places to sings hymns in praise of him. This is followed by the distribution of prasad or holy food. While some households and public places immerse the idol after a day, others keep it for five days, seven days, or the entire ten days. During this period, devotees abstain from eating meat or consuming liquor. Households that bring an idol of Lord Ganesha invite family members, friends, and other associates to their homes for taking the blessings of Ganesha. On the day of immersion, people bid a tearful adieu to the lord and urge him to return next year through songs and mantras. The idols are immersed in the ocean, lake, canal, or one of the several eco-friendly spots created throughout the country for the purpose of idol immersion.

The public celebration of Ganesh Chaturthi can be traced to the Maratha Kingdom in Pune during the era of Maratha ruler Shivaji Raje Bhosale in the seventeenth century. The peshawas or royal caretakers or administrators continued its traditions. Since they worshipped Ganesha as their kula devata or family/clan god, they erected several temples in his honor. Once the Maratha Empire crashed, the festival lost its momentum. It wasn't celebrated with as much glory and grandeur as it was during the era of the Maratha rule.

However, Bal Gangadhar Tilak, a social reformist and Indian freedom fighter, restarted the practice of public celebrations of

Ganesha Chaturthi. He saw this as a wonderful opportunity to get people together against the oppressive British regime. Tilak sought to inculcate values of unity, brotherhood, and nationalism in Indians, which would encourage them to participate in the freedom movement. Under his guidance and initiative, devotees began to install huge images and idols of Lord Ganesha throughout city pavilions during the festival. They also carried these idols in large processions amidst chants of "Ganpati Bappa Morya" through crowded streets before finally immersing them in water bodies. From the Maratha Empire and Maharashtra, the festival gradually gained prominence throughout the country and subcontinent, with Indians celebrating the festival across the world today.

The first day is considered to be the most important day of Ganesha Chaturthi, where the deity is brought to the house or public place amidst much fanfare. From the time of invocation until he is immersed, Ganesha is worshipped with plenty of respect and devotion. Once the idol is installed in public places, worshippers continue to throng them and pay homage to the elephant god, while participating in celebrations and festivities. In addition to the pomp and revelry, the festival also helps generate plenty of business, buying, and commercial activity.

On the first day, the worship may last for a few hours early in the morning. The invocation puja is either performed by the household members themselves or helmed by a priest. The priest will offer elaborate instructions about the materials that will be needed to perform different rituals. The advantage of engaging priests is that they are known to recite prayers and mantras accurately while ensuring all rituals are correctly observed. However, nowadays, many modern Hindu households denounce the practice of employing the serves of priests and perform all the rituals themselves.

The worship and puja of Ganesha is a fairly elaborate ritual that is based on the smarta philosophy and tradition. It is followed in pretty much the same way that worship of other deities is observed. The main objective is to invite the god the way you would invite a guest to your house, honoring him with love, hospitality, and attention. To begin, you would offer water to clean their hands and feet, water for drinking purposes, and a relaxing, comfortable place to sit. Later, arrangements would be made for their bathing, food, and clothes. This is followed by having pleasant conversations with the guest through chants, mantras, and prayers, while the guest relishes his food and the attention that is given to him. Finally, when it is time for him to return, he thanks you for the hospitality and devotion by showering you with blessings, wishes, and happiness. This is exactly how Ganesh Chaturthi is traditionally celebrated.

Conclusion

Thank you for making it through to the end of *Hinduism: What You Need to Know about the Hindu Religion, Gods, Goddesses, Beliefs, History, and Rituals.* It should have been informative and provided you with all the tools that you need to achieve your goals, whatever they may be.

Just because you have finished this book doesn't mean that there is nothing left to learn on this topic. Expanding your horizons is the only way to find the mastery in which you seek.

The next step is to stop reading and ask yourself if you have decided that Hinduism is the religion for you. If so, begin your practice with the simple question: What is it that will bring me to my place of enlightenment and achieve Moksha? Even though there are many facets to Hinduism, all of these parts are united by that one simple answer of achieving enlightenment through recognizing your duty to live your best life. The tricky part is answering it for you. If you have enjoyed learning about Hinduism, you may also enjoy learning about Buddhism and Jainism as both have similar threads to Hinduism.

Here's another book by Crystal Moon you might like

Thanks again for reading *Hinduism What You Need to Know about the Hindu Religion, Gods, Goddesses, Beliefs, History, and Rituals*

If you found this book informative, a review on Amazon would be very much appreciated because it help me a lot!

Made in United States
North Haven, CT
05 November 2022

26308063R00062